# FROM COTTON FIELDS TO BOARD ROOMS

*Best Wishes*

*Joseph Greene*

*Barney Greene*

*January 20, 2008*

## Joseph D. Greene

*From Cotton Fields to Board Rooms*

Published by Hats Off Books®
610 East Delano Street, Suite 104
Tucson, Arizona 85705 U.S.A.
www.hatsoffbooks.com

International Standard Book Number: 1-58736-460-3
Library of Congress Control Number: 2005922025

*This book is dedicated to my wonderful wife, Barney,*
*who has been my devoted partner for forty-three years,*
*to our children, Cathy, Tyrone, David, and Mistey,*
*and our grandchildren, who have brought*
*so much joy to the adventure of life.*

# CONTENTS

# ACKNOWLEDGMENTS

I WISH TO EXPRESS a sincere word of appreciation to all of those who encouraged me as I traveled the winding road of life. From my early years in life, I have received the loving support of family and friends in the Cross-Greene community. The support from the Springfield Baptist Church and the Thomson community has sustained and encouraged me through my many endeavors. The support of friends and colleagues at the Pilgrim Health and Life Insurance Company and at Augusta State University has been a source of strength.

A well-deserved thanks is extended to my graduate assistant, Michele Brown. Michele did a great job of reading, typing, and proofing draft after draft.

Finally, I am grateful to my loving wife, Barney, for her continued support and encouragement. To these, and so many unnamed people, I am humbly grateful.

*Chapter One*

# COTTON FIELDS

THE COTTON FIELDS IN rural Emanuel County seemed endless. The temperature seemed unbearably hot. Seemed as though there was no way to escape the grueling job of picking cotton from sunup until sundown. Being born to loving parents, Charlie and Lula Greene, did not shelter me from the cotton fields in rural Emanuel County. In fact, as their oldest child, much more work was expected of me. My role was to set an example for my siblings. An example of hard work and determination that would lead to a life of unlimited opportunity and success. In my mind, though, life on the farm and the cotton fields offered a bleak future and little opportunity, except to dream of better days to come. My dreams were enormous. Under the blistering sun of the cotton fields, I dreamed of things, places, and opportunities that were far removed from my reach. To my parents' credit, they did not dash my dreams. Perhaps they were their dreams too.

The Greene family's roots are deep in the rural soil of Emanuel County, Georgia. My grandfather, Winder Greene, was an unusual man. He owned land in an era when most African-Americans did not own land. That is, most African-Americans were sharecroppers. Grandpa not only owned land but, according to older relatives, he was also rather radical and independent. So forceful was Grandpa that he held off the Ku Klux Klan by himself with guns and gunpowder bombs when they came to his home to terrorize his family. My parents moved in with Grandpa when he became too ill to take care of himself, and they lived with Grandpa until he died. My

1

father's mother, Carrie Hagen Greene, died when my father was twelve years old, and Grandpa remained unmarried. Grandpa kept me during the day while my parents worked in the fields. He read newspapers to me and I would tear the papers into bits and pieces. My relatives said that Grandpa had a special love for me and allowed me to do things that others dared not do.

Upon Grandpa's death, his property was divided among his seven children. He gave the house to my parents, along with the surrounding land. Although property lines were drawn to separate the parcels of land, the Greene family worked cooperatively together without regard for the legal lines of division. This spirit of family unity had a compelling influence on me as I grew up watching my parents, aunts, uncles, and cousins sharing and working together as one family.

During this era in rural Emanuel County, there were no public schools for African-Americans who lived some distance from the school in the city of Swainsboro, Georgia. My family lived twenty miles from the city of Swainsboro, and there weren't any buses to transport the students to the city. In response to the situation that they found themselves in, the Greene family erected a family school to educate their children. Another large black family in the area, the Cross family, built a school for their children as well. These schools were modest at best. Importantly though, these families' sacrifices spoke volumes about the importance of education. They wanted their future generations to enjoy opportunities that had been denied them.

## Cross-Greene School

In 1944 the two families, the Cross family and the Greene family, pooled their resources and built a school for the community. The school was named Cross-Greene School. My father, along with uncles and other relatives, worked months in constructing the school. When I was a young five-year-old child, my mother would send my father's lunch in a gallon pail with my sister Christine and me. As we approached the site, we could hear the hammers and laughter as they proudly built a school for their children. As a child of only five, I knew that education was important because my father, uncles, and older relatives worked on the school. Uncle James shared a story with me during his illness before his death about the difficulty they had in constructing the school. They used mules and wagons to transport lumber and other building supplies from Swainsboro to the building site, which was approximately twenty miles away. Uncle James and others negotiated with suppliers to extend discounted prices and credit. In some instances, they used rejected lumber and second-grade materials. The school was constructed on a parcel of land donated by Mr. Durden. He was an African-American who had acquired a substantial amount of land. Mr. Durden owned a grocery store near the site, which was close to Piney Grove Baptist Church. The school was constructed of red bricks and concrete floors.

I was excited about going to school. The problem was that the school was not finished in time for the new school year. Arrangements were made for us to attend school at the family's church, Piney Grove Baptist Church, until the school was completed. The first few days at Piney Grove were hectic in that the church was small and had no walls to separate the classes by grade. The teachers, being resourceful, used bed lining to hang as partition walls to separate the classes. The teachers used their own discretion for bathroom breaks and recess. Shortly we were ready to move to Cross-Greene school, which was a very short distance from the church. For me, it seemed thousands of miles away as I enjoyed every moment of the newness of the school. I continued at Cross-Greene until I finished the eighth grade. By this time, the Emanuel County school system had begun to provide a bus to transport the children to Swainsboro to attend high school. Having transportation to Swainsboro meant that the Cross-Greene School would close a few years later.

My years at Cross-Greene were exciting. I walked one mile to school every day from our home. The school was modest at best. We had outside toilets, and no running water or lunchroom. The school was heated with charcoals in an iron potbelly stove in each classroom. The boys were responsible for bringing coals in every morning and starting the fire. The girls had chores as well. They swept the floors and cleaned the rooms. I participated in school activities and was a champion speller during the annual spelling bee contest. I also got into trouble at school. The boys would climb into the loft and jump from rafter to rafter. One day during this dangerous activity, a boy missed the rafter and fell through the ceiling, landing on the floor in the building. Our principal, Mr. Thomas, had all the boys in the school line up for confessions. Although I was not at school during the time of the accident—I had gone to Swainsboro to participate in a school radio broadcast—someone told Mr. Thomas that I had been in the loft in the past. When I returned to school, I noticed that the boys were strangely quiet and subdued. After Mr. Thomas sent for me, I quickly found out why the boys were in such a passive mood as Mr. Thomas whipped me with his belt. I was so afraid that my sister, Christine, would tell my father. If my father found out about my adventures at school, I would get another whipping … no questions asked. My parents supported the teachers. They did not second-guess their decisions, especially on matters of discipline. Our teachers were hardworking, dedicated teachers. They had limited resources, very little pay, and substandard conditions. One of my teachers, Ms. Irene McClain, had also taught my father. She was well past the normal retirement age. Ms. McClain was a strict disciplinarian. During one of my classes under Ms. Irene, as we referred to her, I attempted to gain laughter from my classmates by making a smart remark to her. She told my father about my remark. My father never asked me to explain my comments; he just took his belt and starting whipping me while reminding me that teachers were to be respected and revered.

The Cross-Greene school afforded its students with all of the opportunities and activities available under the depressed economic conditions of the era. We had an outside basketball court, a sand pit, and a smooth surface area where the boys could shoot marbles. My mother would fuss at me about my trousers being dirty from playing in the sand and shooting marbles. During the spring, we were permitted to take our shoes off and go to school without shoes. This allowed me an opportunity to wade in the stream on the road between my home and the school. I participated in the school's dramatic plays, spelling bees, and other literary programs. Although I loved basketball, I was never good at the game. I agonized over my inability to participate as a varsity player.

Finally, it was time for me to graduate from Cross-Greene and take the big leap to Emanuel County High School as a ninth grader. Emanuel County High School was located in Swainsboro, Georgia, approximately twenty miles from Cross-Greene. A school bus was provided to transport the students to high school. I was struck with awe when I got to the high school. The school was relatively new, with indoor plumbing and a lunchroom. Black students were there from various communities in Emanuel County. We were, in some respect, considered outsiders. Unlike the kids who lived in Swainsboro, we were bused in from smaller rural communities and towns. We did not know the teachers, the surroundings, or the "hip" behavior of city kids. Many of the kids who had grown up in Swainsboro teased us for being "country hicks." We were placed in class sections, thus some of my classmates from Cross-Greene were not in my classes. I am not sure how the teachers determined how the classes were to be separated. At any rate, I was placed in class 9-A, where I gradually made new friends with kids from other sections of Emanuel County. There were students from Cross-Greene, Twin City, Stillmore, Summertown, Oakgrove, and other small towns and communities. Students were bused in from the various communities in Emanuel County.

Emanuel County High School was new. Throughout the state of Georgia, flat-top schools were built for black students. These schools were built in response to the separate-but-equal law that was being challenged before the Supreme Court. In an attempt to avoid school integration, school boards engaged in a massive construction program. These schools had lunchrooms and inside plumbing. Because of my family's economic conditions, I rarely had lunch money. However, I had lunch. Mr. Nick, the school janitor, would allow some of the boys to assist him in cleaning the lunchroom in exchange for lunch. He permitted me to work daily. I had to wait until all the students had been served before I could eat. On a few occasions, the food ran out and I did not have any to eat. However, more often, I had more than I could eat because we could have all of the leftovers.

My bus picked me up at 7:30 a.m., and we usually arrived at 8:30 a.m. I enjoyed social studies, history, English, literature, and biology. I did not like algebra and my grades showed that I did not like algebra. Our books were secondhand books. They were old books that had been used by the white students at Swainsboro High. Many of the books were torn with missing pages. We only had one microscope in the science lab. Therefore, we were not allowed to experiment and play around with the microscope. Our science teacher, Mr. Swain, would set up an experiment field on the microscope and we were allowed to look at the experiment and comment on what we saw. Our teachers never complained about the lack of resources. They challenged us to take advantage of the few things that we had at school.

The daily bus ride from Cross-Greene to Emanuel County High was preceded by a host of early morning chores. I milked two cows, Dollie and Little Gal, gathered wood for the cooking stove and the fireplace, and brought in water from the outside well. My Saturdays were busy too. My father's barn held the supply of corn to take us through the winter months. The corn had to be shucked and shelled on Saturday so that my father could take it to the corn mill in Wadley, Georgia. The shelled corn was ground into cornmeal and grits. Our daily meal consisted of grits and corn bread. My father's smokehouse provided a source of some good eating. The smoked hams from the butchered hogs were an enjoyable source of food. My parents pretty much grew or raised everything that we ate. My mother canned enough vegetables from the garden to take us through the winter months. While the daily diet of pork and fat would not satisfy today's nutritional diet, it kept us fed and full. My family did not have indoor plumbing, running water, or electricity. I remember how excited I was when electricity was installed at our house. I stared at the light bulb in utter disbelief. My uncle James was the first person in our community to have a small black and white television and a telephone. My father was a boxing fan, which meant that on Wednesday nights we would go to Uncle James's house to watch boxing. At other times, my father and I would listen to boxing on our radio at our home. My father was a big fan of Joe Louis and would drop all chores when Louis fought in order to listen to every blow. I did not realize the gravity of poverty that we were experiencing. I only knew that we had plenty of food, fire burning in the fireplace to keep us from freezing, a wagon and mule to take us to church, a change of clothing, and loving parents.

My summer days were filled with fun. After we finished working in the cotton fields, we were off to our favorite fishing hole. My father loved to fish and he made sure that my cousins and I were tagging along. We fished in several creeks near our home and enjoyed the fish that we caught. There were times when we fished all night in the Ogeechee River. My father would build a large fire as we gathered for a night of fishing. He would bring cornmeal for frying the fish, bread, and canned peaches. He fried the fish over an open fire in a large can. We generally caught catfish and eel at night. My father seemed to have as much fun as we did. We would compete to see who would catch the largest fish. The next morning we would return home, where we were greeted by family members who were anxious to examine our catch.

During the winter months, we would hunt for rabbits, squirrels, and raccoons. My father, again, would lead a delegation of cousins and myself into the woods. Some of the nights were so cold that I would shiver and shake. My father, who stood over six feet, was well built and strong. My uncle James, however, had suffered a crippling injury and could not navigate the woods. Years earlier he and my father were doing some logging work and a tree fell on my uncle James and fractured his leg. The leg was not properly treated, which resulted in the leg becoming immobile. My uncle Charlie was well up in age and could not move too well in rugged terrain, although he would take us fishing on occasion. Thus my father, stronger and younger, would take all of my uncles' boys and me fishing and hunting frequently.

Sundays were fun days too. We always went to church on Sunday. We were members of the Piney Grove Baptist Church. Piney Grove was approximately one mile from our home. Before my father purchased a car, we rode to church in a mule-drawn wagon. Most of the Greene family members were members of Piney Grove. My great grandfather, Solomon Greene, was one of the organizers of the church. I became an usher at Piney Grove; my cousin James, Jr. and I were the first male ushers at our church. Following church services, we would return home for the best meal of the week. My mother would prepare fried chicken and a host of vegetables. Later in the afternoon, my cousins and I would gather for a game of baseball or basketball. The routine was predictable; we did the same thing Sunday after Sunday, year after year. Christmas was very special too. Although we were extremely poor, my parents managed to provide us with a limited number of toys at Christmas. The Greene family would visit and share food on Christmas. We would walk to Uncle James and Aunt Pearlie's home, return, and visit Uncle Charlie and Aunt Lizzie before the day was over. They in turn would do the same, making stops at our home too.

## Family Breakup

My sister, Christine, and I were very close. She was two years younger than I was. Since we were the only children that my parents had at that time, Christine followed me through the fields, climbed trees, and played the games that I liked. When it was time for me to start school at age six, Christine, who was four, cried to go along with me to school. My brother, Solomon, was born when I was eight years old. Christine and I were so excited about his birth that we wanted to hold him and feed him. I remember kissing him on his cheek and holding his small hands. Meanwhile, my parents were growing apart without my realizing what was happening. They would argue for extended periods of time. I did not realize that my family was on the brink of breaking up until the day my father moved away from home. I was very sad and felt that my world was coming apart. Neither my mother nor father discussed the situation with Christine and me. On one occasion, I got up enough courage to ask my father to explain to me why he and my mother had separated. He simply said, "That's none of your business." Knowing my father as I did, I dropped the issue. He was not a man of many words. When he spoke, people would take note because he meant what he said. His leaving my mother was not abandonment of his family. My father would make frequent visits to our home to bring food, give us some spending money, inquire about our progress in school, and tell us about the importance of education.

One day out of the blue, my father told my sister and me that he was taking custody of the three of us and that our mother would be leaving to live with her sister, Mary, in Philadelphia. Sure enough, my aunt Mary arrived and my mother packed her belongings and left for Philadelphia with her. My father returned to live with us in the family home. He also brought a lady with him, Mattie Lee, who would become my stepmother. I resented her moving in with us and did not get off to a good relationship with her. My sister, Christine, started referring to her as Mama. I refused to call her Mama and insisted on calling her Miss Mattie Lee. My brother, Solomon, who was less than two years old, called her Mama. Miss Mattie Lee and I did not get along very well. I grew to accept her as my father's wife, but not as my mother. My mother, who was now living in Philadelphia, kept in touch with us through the mail. Following every letter from my mother, my father would insist on Christine and me writing to my mother in return.

He would often tell us to always remember our mother and remind us that their differences should not affect our love for our mother.

*Chapter Two*

# FUTURE PLANS

ONE DAY DURING MY senior year in high school, as my father and I walked near the barn, he asked me if I wanted to go to college. He said that he did not have any money, but would see if he could borrow some if I wanted to go off to college. Although I wanted to go to college, I knew that he did not have any money or any means of borrowing money. I said that instead of college, I would apply for a job with the Pilgrim Health and Life Insurance Company, and that perhaps he could scrape up enough money to send Christine to college when she finished high school later. I sensed that my father was hurt and disappointed that he did not have the resources to send me to college. There were not many kids from our area who went off to college. My cousin, Carrie Greene, had gone to Savannah State College. She was an inspiring cousin who seemed to have a wealth of knowledge and to know every-thing that was important. I would listen to her and my older cousins in the summer months as we picked cotton in the fields. I wanted to know as much as Carrie knew about the world.

My family had insurance with the Pilgrim Health and Life Insurance Company. Mr. William Dukes, a company salesman, serviced our area. He would inquire about my schoolwork and would challenge me to get good grades. Mr. Dukes would often tell me that he wanted me to take his job when I finished high school. I admired Mr. Dukes's professionalism, his busi-ness attire, and his new cars. I would daydream of having a job like Mr. Dukes. His job would take me far away from the cotton fields of Emanuel County. Upon graduation from high school, I told Mr. Dukes that I was ready for his job. He responded by saying, "Well, I am not ready to retire, but I will help you get a job with Pilgrim, and if you get the job, remember that the only thing that Pilgrim will owe you is an opportunity, and what you make of it is up to you." He gave me an employment application with instructions to send it off as soon as possible.

## Farewell to Cotton Fields

I anxiously and nervously completed the employment application that Mr. Dukes had given me for employment with Pilgrim. The application also required a cover letter to accompany the employment application. I asked my cousin Carrie, who was completing her degree at Savannah State College, to review my application letter and to make the necessary corrections. With the letter mailed off to Pilgrim, I returned to the cotton fields to earn some much-needed money. The days seemed to stretch into years while I anxiously waited for a reply from Pilgrim. I dreamed of leaving the blistering sun and the backbreaking work of picking cotton. There were days when I thought that perhaps I should have gone with my father and my cousins Rufus and John Henry to work as a migrant worker picking apples in upstate New York. My father had started traveling to New York in late summer to earn money picking apples, and to Florida in the winter to pick citrus fruits. He had asked me if I wanted to travel with them to New York to earn some money while I was waiting to hear from Pilgrim. I declined the offer and elected to stay in Cross-Greene and pick cotton so that I would be in a position to quickly accept an employment opportunity with Pilgrim. Finally, a letter came from Pilgrim. I was too nervous to open it immediately. The letter informed me that I had been accepted to attend the company's sales academy. I was to report to Pilgrim's home office in Augusta, Georgia on September 14, 1959 at 8:00 a.m. I was so excited and told everyone who would listen to me about my having been accepted by Pilgrim as an employee. I made arrangements with the pastor of Piney

Grove Baptist Church, Reverend G. H. Wingfield, to ride with him to Augusta. Reverend Wingfield lived in Augusta and would be at Piney Grove on the second Sunday of the month for our regular second Sunday worship services. With my $35 saved from picking cotton, one Sunday suit of clothes, a couple of dress shirts and trousers, and a million-dollar smile on my face, I was off to pursue a career in the life insurance industry.

Early Monday morning on September 14, 1959, Reverend Wingfield dropped me off at the corporate office of the Pilgrim Health and Life Insurance Company in Augusta, Georgia. As I stood and looked at the large marble and masonry building, 1143 Gwinnett Street, of Pilgrim's headquarters, I was frightened and struck with awe. A part of me wanted to return to the friendly confines of Cross-Greene. This was only the second time that I had been away from home. I did not know what to expect. Would I measure up to Pilgrim's expectations? How could I go from cotton picker to insurance representative? Someone directed me to the training facility with instructions to make myself comfortable. Pretty soon, I discovered that there were nine young men who had been accepted for the sales academy. Mr. M. M. Scott, Sr., dean of the school, warmly greeted us and covered the details of the training program. We would be in school for nine weeks, covering the many facets of insurance. We would also sit for the state insurance examination during our final week. We were admonished that if we failed the state examination, we would return to our respective homes, unemployed. We would be rooming in private homes of people with whom Pilgrim had arranged accommodations. I was assigned to Mrs. Hattie Thompson's home. The company paid me $35 per week. Following deductions for taxes and supplies, I had $26 left. From this amount, I paid $10 per week to Mrs. Thompson for rooming expenses and allowed $10 per week for food. On weekends, I would catch the city bus to visit with Reverend and Mrs. Wingfield. During my visits, I would give Mrs. Wingfield $5 per week to save for me. My roommate was Fred Robbins from Midway, Alabama. Fred stood about 5'3", which meant that I was one foot taller at 6'3". Our classmates called us Mutt and Jeff. Mrs.

Thompson's home was one block from Pilgrim's office, which made it quite convenient for us in that we did not own cars. Fred and I shared one bed at Mrs. Thompson's until we graduated from the academy.

Most of my Pilgrim classmates were college graduates and older. They treated Fred and me as though we were younger brothers. Mr. Scott, dean of the school, was a senior officer with Pilgrim with many years of experience. He was an inspiring teacher. He taught us much about life insurance, but much more about life. I sat in awe as he lectured to us daily. Mr. Scott's superior, Jim Hinton, Sr., was the company's agency director in charge of field operations. Upon graduation from the sales academy, we would be working under Mr. Hinton's directions. Mr. Hinton was an intimidating man who had a reputation as a strict disciplinarian. He had served in the military as an officer and treated everyone as though they were his subordinates in military uniforms. We feared him and would be on our best behavior whenever he visited the class. Upon graduation, we would be assigned to various areas of the company's field operations. I was assigned to Mr. E. G. Long, Sr. in Thomson, Georgia for my field training. Mr. Long had enjoyed a long illustrious career with Pilgrim as one of their top agents. My role was to learn from his vast wealth of field experience and to ultimately be assigned somewhere else.

## *Thomson to Become Home*

I reported to Mr. Long on November 2, 1959. When I arrived at his home, he took me to a house on Shank Street, where I was to room with Mrs. Adline Hardwick at $5 per week. Mrs. Hardwick was an older lady who had strict house rules. I had saved $45, which led me to opening my first bank account. Mr. Long took me to the Bank of Thomson where I opened an account. I bought a small stereo record player and a couple of 45" records. Mrs. Hardwick informed me that if I played the record player at her house my rent would increase by $5.00 per week to offset the additional use of electricity. While I did not say anything to Mrs. Hardwick, I complained to Mr. and Mrs. Long about the additional charge. Mrs. Long responded by saying that if I did not mind sharing a room with her two sons, Donald and Edward, I could move to their home. I quickly packed my belongings and moved to Ellington Avenue with the Long family. In moving in with the Longs, I was able to eat and sleep for $10 per week.

The Long family was a loving and caring family. They had four children. Their daughter, Edwina, was attending college in Alabama. Donald, Joyce, and Edward were still in grade school. Mrs. Long was a teacher with the McDuffie County school system. They were prominent members of the Thomson community and members of the Springfield Baptist Church. The Longs were very active in the church and community. They treated me as though I was a member of their family and supported my growth and development. For instance, during the long daily rides in the car with Mr. Long, he lectured me on life's values and proper relationships with members of the opposite sex. He cautioned me about people I should not associate with and why some people would not be conducive for my career development. Mr. Long was devoted to the Springfield Baptist Church. He was a deacon, Sunday School teacher, and one of the key leaders in the church. I quickly became active at the Springfield Baptist Church. Naturally, I became involved in Sunday school and the Baptist Training Union.

Springfield was under the leadership of the Reverend J. H. West. He was an inspiring leader, with a solid education from Morehouse College. His leadership in the community extended beyond the walls of the church. His wife, Clara West, was a professor at Fort Valley State College and quite a leader as well. I looked forward to going to church on Sundays to listen to his inspiring sermons. His messages were excellent signposts not only for the route to heaven, but also through the pathway of life on Earth.

I worked hard under Mr. Long and saved money weekly from my paychecks. I eventually saved enough money to purchase a car. I purchased a used 1956 Chevrolet for $1,095, with a down payment of $200. My monthly payments were $51 per month. Mr. Long provided me with valuable advice on the proper use and maintenance of the car. Meanwhile, Mrs. West learned of my desire to purchase some land. She offered to sell me a lot on Whitehead Street for $250. I agreed to buy the parcel of land, which represented my first purchase of land and a depletion of all the money that I had saved. I was very proud of my decision to buy the land. I had learned at an early age the value of land and how the ownership of land represented a sound investment.

I met a man who was later to become one of my best friends. North Carolina Mutual Life Insurance Company sent a young representative, Rhennevor Gloster, to establish a block of business in the Thomson area. While we were competitors, we quickly became close friends. Rhennevor had recently graduated from Paine College and was sincere about his career. He had aspirations to become the top salesman with his company. We would spend hours discussing our plans and strategizing on marketing techniques. Deep inside of me I was determined to reach the pinnacle of success before Rhennevor did. I always had the feeling that he felt the same way toward me. He and I would compete daily in the field against each other and socialize together when we were off. Neither Rhennevor nor I socialized much. We would go the movies occasionally and to the American Legion Post on Teachers' Night. Most of the time we would sit and talk about our plans. I admired his devotion to his company and his work ethic. His coming to Thomson was good for me. His coming kept me focused on my career and fueled my desire to become the number one agent with Pilgrim.

After several months of being under the supervision of Mr. Long, the company decided to let me remain in Thomson and establish a block of business independent of Mr. Long's block of business. I was to build a block of business from scratch. I was not to solicit in homes where Mr. Long had business relationships. I was excited about the prospects of being independent. This was also an opportunity for me to earn commissions and to expand my income. By now, I knew my way around Thomson and knew where there were sales opportunities that were not being serviced by Mr. Long. I was assigned to Leo Jackson's staff as his rookie. Leo was a supportive supervisor. He always found ways to compliment my efforts and to motivate me to do more. Within weeks of being solo, my sales performance was gaining notice in the company. I started to receive congratulatory letters from some of Pilgrim's senior officers, including Mr. Hinton. My name was published in the company's monthly publication and I soon discovered that I had won the company's Rookie Salesman of the Year award. During the company's annual participation in the National Insurance Association's Sales Week, I won top honors in that as well. I gained confidence in my abilities and began to feel secure about my career and my earning potential with Pilgrim.

*Chapter Three*

# THE LADY OF MY LIFE

BEING A YOUNG BACHELOR in Thomson was exciting for a period of time. I received calls and notes for dates from young ladies that I did not even know. As time went on, I began to think long term. I began to pray and ask God to send someone into my life who would become my soul mate for life. Sure enough, a young lady from South Carolina came to Thomson to teach school for one year. She was the daughter of a friend of the principal of the black high school, who had been recruited to complete one school term. The school term was already underway and the principal, Mr. Norris, convinced her to come to Thomson for one year only. I met my future wife shortly after she arrived in Thomson. She was brought to Mr. and Mrs. Long's home to room with another young lady who was also rooming with the Long family. Barney was quiet and conscientious about her work as a teacher. She and I engaged in small talk with no obvious interest beyond conversation. Months later, she and I began dating. Once we began dating, I knew that she was the person who I wanted to marry. She was a caring person who cared so much for her students. She was an honest, hardworking, gentle person who wanted to spend her life helping others. I proposed to her, and to my delight, she accepted my proposal to marry her. I traveled to her home, Wagener, South Carolina, to ask her parents' permission to marry her. They were gracious and consented. Her father was quite an entrepreneur. He owned a funeral home, a grocery store, and a relatively large farm. He was such a quiet, gentle man who had devoted much of his life to serving and helping people in all walks of life. Barney and I were married August 13, 1961. Rhennevor Gloster was my best man. Rhennevor was more conservative than I was. He could stretch a dollar far beyond imagination. Prior to the wedding, I gave Rhennevor $10 to give to the minister, Rev. L. M. Tyler, for performing the wedding ceremony. Following the wedding reception, Rhennevor handed me $5 and said, "Put that in your pocket." I asked him where he had gotten the money from. He said, "I only gave that preacher $5; you need the money more than he does."

Although we received several wedding gifts, the one that sticks out in my mind is the gift that we received from Mr. Hinton. Having given an impression of being an unemotional man at Pilgrim, he sent us a very warm congratulatory letter along with a check for five dollars. We used the five dollars to open our first joint-savings account, which became our catalyst for financial independence.

Upon returning to Thomson from our wedding, we rented an apartment from the Long family for two months while our home was constructed on the parcel of land that I had purchased earlier from Mrs. West. Our budget was extremely tight. Barney was earning little more than $200 per month teaching, and my sales earnings were about the same. Our mortgage payment was $78, car payment $51, and furniture payments $50 per month. To supplement our income, we took in a boarder, and I did substitute teaching at the various county schools. Still, we managed to save a small amount from our earnings every month.

We led simple lives as a married couple. Occasionally we went to the movies at the Martin Theater in Thomson. The theater was segregated. African-Americans had to sit in the balcony and could not use the restrooms. This practice of racial segregation was common in the south at most public facilities, including segregated water fountains and restrooms at the McDuffie County Courthouse.

Barney and I always attended worship services at the Springfield Baptist Church. I also served as a Sunday school teacher at Springfield. Following worship services, we would return to our home on Whitehead Street and have our special

Sunday dinner. Dinner was followed by our reading and watching television on our small black and white television set.

We usually visited Barney's parents in Wagener, South Carolina once a month on a weekend. The drive to Wagener from Thomson was about two hours. We generally drove to Wagener late Saturday afternoon after I had completed my insurance service and collection calls. Most of my clients were weekly wage earners who paid their bills weekly. Therefore, in order for me to keep their insurance coverage from lapsing for nonpayment, I visited their homes and collected their premiums on Fridays and Saturdays. Barney would accompany me on some occasions as I made my calls to my client's homes.

Although we were not earning much money, we managed to save a small amount monthly. Barney was supportive and made many budgetary sacrifices as we struggled to establish a financial base. We only had one car, a 1957 Chevrolet; Barney would catch a ride with our neighbors Calvin and Mary Sampson or others to work. She was unselfish and endured the sacrifices without complaining.

As our young marriage gained solid footing, so did my career with Pilgrim. Through long hours of hard work, I established name recognition within the company as one of their top agents. My name appeared in a top leadership position in the company's performance publication. I won awards and citations as a leading agent with Pilgrim.

## Corporate Move

Mr. M. M. Scott, Vice President and Dean of Pilgrim's training department, had keenly followed my development with Pilgrim. He approached me in 1962 about changing my career path with the company from sales to management. I was quite excited about the prospect of moving up the corporate ladder with Pilgrim. One problem, though: I would be required to leave Thomson and join Mr. Scott on the road. Mr. Scott was vice president—associate agency director. I would accompany him on the road as he traveled throughout the four states that Pilgrim was licensed in to promote marketing and sales operations. Although Barney did not relish the idea of my being gone five days a week, she was supportive of my career development. She never complained.

Being on the road was not easy. The areas that we traveled in were segregated. We could not live in the hotels and motels. Instead, we lived in private homes that accommodated business travelers. The restaurants were segregated too. Some of them would not even serve African-Americans in separate dining rooms. Mr. Scott (Skipper) was the most captivating man that I had met. He did not express any negative feelings about anyone or anything. He was a storehouse of motivation. A graduate of Paine College, he played football as a lineman in college at barely over 125 pounds. He taught and preached to me night and day about pursuing your dreams. He pounded into me over and over again about the value of an education. Mr. Scott often referred to the men who were under his supervisions as "Hoss." He said to me: "Hoss, I want you to go back to school and complete your education; you never know what may happen to Pilgrim." Deep inside of me, I always wanted to go to college. I often played back my father's conversation with me about attending college. While I was making progress in my management development, I felt as though something was missing.

After a year on the road with Mr. Scott, I was given a region to direct on my own, as a regional supervisor in North Georgia. I was responsible for marketing and sales development in our district offices in Atlanta, Athens, Macon, Columbus, and Griffin, Georgia. My duties required me to travel to these offices weekly. I normally left Thomson early on Monday and returned on Friday.

During the summer of 1965, Dr. Lemuel Penn, an African-American educator and Army reserve officer from Washington, D.C., upon completing Reserve duty at Fort Benning, Georgia, headed home via Athens, Georgia. He would never make it home to his family. As he and some fellow military officers drove through rural Georgia near Athens, he was gunned down. It was reported that he and his fellow officers stopped to get some gasoline at a rural service station near Athens, where there was purported to have been Klan activity. There was suspicion that some members of the Ku Klux Klan had committed the crime. The incident made national headlines because Mr. Penn was a leader in the Washington, D.C. school system. An extensive federal investigation was launched, and racial tensions in that area were extremely high. When traveling in the area, I exercised extreme caution. I did not make any stops, and I was careful to observe the posted speed limits. One night as I was returning from Toccoa, Georgia from a meeting with one our sales representatives, I drove through the small city of Bowman, Georgia. As I stopped at the traffic light, I took note of the fact that there was a crowd of men standing near the street. I drove slowly through the city and observed that a car was following me. I became concerned as I reflected on the recent murder of the military officer in the same vicinity. After driving about one mile, the car pulled up close to my Volkswagen with a flashing police light on. I pulled over as a policeman approached me. The policeman asked, "Boy, where are you going?" I told him that I was returning home from work. "Why did you come through my town speeding?" he said. I responded by saying, "Officer, I was not speeding." He placed his hand on his pistol and said, "I say that you were speeding." I responded by saying, "I am sorry." The policeman then said, "That's more like it. … Now, nigger, I don't want you to come through my town speeding again, and I want you to tell niggers that you know to stay out of my town. Now get outta here." I nervously drove off while thanking God that the policeman did not shoot me.

The encounter with the policeman was nothing compared to another incident near Toccoa, Georgia. In August of 1965, as I traveled toward Toccoa to meet with our agent, I was involved in an accident that nearly cost me my life. A driver of a logging truck failed to stop as he crossed U.S. 17. His truck hit my Volkswagen, sending me down a deep embankment, pinned in my car. Thank God that I was wearing my seatbelt. The driver of the logging truck did not offer any help. He left the scene of the accident. Fortunately, a lady who came upon the accident called for help. The Stephens County Hospital sent an ambulance to the scene, only to discover that they had sent the "whites only" ambulance. The driver decided that in order to save my life, he would not wait for the hospital to send the "colored" ambulance. He transported me to the hospital in the wrong ambulance. When I regained consciousness at the hospital, the nurses shared the story with me about how I had broken the color barrier in Stephens County, Georgia.

*Chapter Four*

# MILITARY SERVICE

UPON RETURNING HOME FROM an assignment in Macon, Georgia, I opened a letter from the United States Selective Service Draft Board. I was to report for induction into the United States Army, August 10, 1966. Although I felt that I had escaped military service due to my age, the Vietnam War had created a manpower shortage. My wife, Barney, was quite upset. We were deeply in debt and had plans that would have to be placed on hold. I tried to show strength in the face of the circumstances.

Upon boarding the bus for the Reception Center in Atlanta, I sat in the middle of the bus. The bus driver reminded me that I should move to the back of the bus and leave those seats for white patrons who might board the bus later. The ride to the reception center seemed forever. My mind reflected on my being discriminated against in all walks of life. My thoughts raced back to the day five years earlier when Rhennevor and I walked into the McDuffie County courthouse to register to vote. The registrar, Myrtis McCorkle, informed us that because we were Negroes, we would have to take a literacy test. She was abusive and called me "nigger" when I did not say "Yes, ma'am" to her when she asked me a question. We had to wait months before we were able to determine whether or not we had passed the literacy test. I kept thinking of how I had been treated as a second-class citizen, yet I was facing the real possibility that my life would be taken in Vietnam in defense of a country that did not accept me as a first-class citizen.

I was sent to Fort Lewis, Washington for basic training. Being three thousand miles away from my family was not an easy assignment. However, I decided that I would make the best of the situation. I was much older than most of the men in my unit and took on the responsibility of trying to become a role model for some of the younger troops. I would become a model soldier and earn the distinction of "Soldier of the Quarter" for my company and my battalion during my tour of duty. Following basic training, I was assigned to Fort Gordon, Georgia for my advance-individualized training as a medical technician. I was excited about being close to home. My sergeant was an understanding man and gave me permission to live off base at home during my training. My being home was welcome news, if only for two months. I received orders to report to Fort Sam Houston, Texas for specialized training as a medic. The training was exciting and I applied myself in learning all that I could learn. Following my graduation from the Basic Medical Corp program, I was given an opportunity to attend the specialized medical training program because I had earned the highest academic average in my military class. When I was summoned to my commander's office, I did not know what to expect. The officer informed me that I was eligible for the advanced training because of my diligent work. Later I realized how God had blessed me in this situation. That is, by the time that I completed the various training programs, I had less than thirteen months in my tour of duty, which meant that I would not be shipped to Vietnam. My next assignment was at Fort Hood, Texas, where I was assigned to Charlie Company, 47th Medical Battalion. My devotion to my work caught the eye of my commanding officer. He assigned me to the office staff as company clerk. I spent most of the time in the office doing clerical work and relaying messages to soldiers who had gotten orders to report to Vietnam.

One day during a visit to the day room, I read a bulletin that changed my direction. The Department of Defense offered free tuition to attend college, at night, under the National Defense Education Act. I was so excited about the prospects of entering college. I enrolled at Mary Harden-Baylor College for evening classes. I tried to recruit several of the men in my unit to take advantage of this opportunity. There was little interest. The last thing they wanted to do at night was to study when they could drink beer and shoot pool. My education got off to a good start. I made an A in my first class, which increased my resolve to continue. It was not easy. I got off from my work assignment at 4:00 p.m., and rushed to the education center for my first class at 5:00 p.m. I usually got back to the barracks around 9:30 p.m. With the lights out in the barracks at 10:00 p.m., I would do my homework in the bathroom while sitting on a toilet. There were nights when I did not finish my homework until after midnight. Some mornings at 5:00 a.m., when I had to get out of the bed for duty, I did not want to continue my pursuit of an education. However, by the time that I was discharged from the army, I had completed my freshman year of college.

The military experience was a sobering experience. There were men in my unit from all regions of the country, with various values. Some of the fellows were deep into drugs, while others were into other vices that would ultimately destroy them. Some were pacifists, militants, homosexuals, racists; some were weak, some strong, and some religious. We were all physically confined to a small world in pursuit of different dreams, different challenges, and ultimately different destinations.

Meanwhile, we traveled together as the war in Vietnam continued to take its toll. The body count of young men who lost their lives in battle continued to grow. Protests against the war in our country continued to escalate. As soldiers, we were bombarded with positive propaganda on the merits of the war and were not allowed to dissent. We were told that those who opposed the war were unpatriotic, or communist. A fellow soldier and I had a heated exchange about the war and Dr. Martin Luther King's opposition to the war. His name was Vansickle, from the state of Kansas. Vansickle told me that Dr. King was a communist because he did not conduct himself as Reverend Billy Graham did. I argued that Dr. King had a right, as a minister, to lead protests against the war, and that it was not fair to brand him a communist. Many of the soldiers in my unit had mixed emotions about our involvement in Vietnam and were quite vocal with their views. I pretty much kept my views to myself, unless I was asked to express them. I felt that the war was pretty much a civil war between the South Vietnamese and the North Vietnamese. I further felt that our involvement in the war was more political than anything else. I felt that our cold war with the Russians had a lot to do with our involvement, and that we feared the Russians' gaining more influence in that region would undermine our global influence. I detested the disproportionate number of African-American men fighting on the front lines and in the jungles in Vietnam. My resentment stemmed from the fact that we had not gained a ride on the front seat of the bus in many American cities or a seat at some lunch counters.

Upon returning to the barracks from my classes on the evening of April 4, 1968, I met a fellow soldier, Mike McCormick from San Francisco, who gave me the sad news. McCormick met me at the door and said, "As a white person, I hate to tell you the sad news, but Dr. Martin Luther King, Jr. has been killed in Memphis, Tennessee." I felt numb and speechless. As I entered the building, some of my fellow soldiers were celebrating Dr. King's death. I became furious over my feelings of helplessness. How should I respond to so many who were filled with so much hate and violence? There were only three African-American soldiers in my unit, who possibly felt the pain that I felt about Dr. King's death. I simply ignored the group and went quietly to my bunk.

The next day my unit was placed on alert. No passes would be extended, nor would anyone be allowed to travel off base, unless absolutely necessary. The military was preparing to respond to civil unrest in some our major urban areas. My unit, the 47th Medical Battalion, started preparing for deployment to a major city in the country to provide medical emergency services. We reviewed procedures and lifesaving techniques. Our secret code was "Garden Plot." On April 6, 1968, we were taken to the airfield for a flight to an unknown city. Once we were loaded on the C-141 transport plane, we were informed that we were headed to Chicago to set up a field hospital to treat injured National Guard soldiers. We arrived in Chicago around 4:00 a.m. where a blistering wind chill met us.

We were taken in military trucks to Grant Park. The open chill was horrific as we worked to erect tents. We were issued M-14 rifles, along with four bullets. Instructions were to shoot only in self-defense. Some of my fellow soldiers in my unit were excited about the prospects of shooting some of those "niggers" as they looted the area. My anger was so intense that I could barely focus on my responsibilities as a medic. The racial epitaphs were loud and frequent. Some of the fellows in my unit did not hide their feelings of hate toward me or any other African-American. During the lunch break the second day we were there, black children from the housing project appeared in large numbers, pressing their faces against the fence that separated us, asking the soldiers to give them some of the fried chicken that we were having for lunch. Some of my fellow soldiers challenged the boys to engage in boxing matches in order to win pieces of chicken. Some of the boys began throwing punches and some of the soldiers began throwing pieces of chicken over the fence. The boys scrambled on the ground to retrieve the chicken. I was furious, and shouted to the soldiers, "Don't throw the chicken to those boys—at least have the decency to hand pieces through the fence." Some of the soldiers laughed and kept throwing the chicken on the ground. My mind was racing with anger. I had thoughts of using some of the bullets that I had been issued on some of my fellow soldiers. I finally turned and walked away as my eyes welled with tears.

After three days in Chicago, we returned to Fort Hood, Texas to resume our regular duties. Although we were back in Texas, the Chicago experience continued to haunt me. I continued to feel hostile toward some of my fellow soldiers. As time passed, my hostilities subsided. I resumed my college studies and kept my mind occupied on schoolwork, books, and reports.

One day during my work in the office of Charlie Company, I was informed that my platoon sergeant had nominated me for "Soldier of the Quarter." This was in recognition of my work performance, leadership, and loyalty. I went through several rounds of competition, winning every round. Finally, the big prize was to win my division's competition. I did not win at this level. However, I was proud of having won my company and my battalion's Soldier of the Quarter designation. This designation earned me some perks and an opportunity to reenlist with a bonus. However, with my having escaped the Vietnam War, I did not give reenlistment a second thought. I felt that I had paid my dues to my country, and that I should concentrate on civilian life. Besides, my wife had made so many sacrifices in trying to manage our financial affairs. There were mortgage payments, a car note, and countless other bills that Barney struggled with during my military tour. My military pay was of little help in paying our bills. However, Barney was quite resourceful and kept things going during my absence. The military experience was rewarding. In two years, I rose through the ranks from an E-1 to the rank of an E-5. Given my military tour, it was time to go home.

*Chapter Five*

# CIVILIAN LIFE AGAIN

THERE WERE SO MANY things that I wanted to do. My career with the Pilgrim Health and Life Insurance Company looked promising. I wanted to continue my education. I wanted to involve myself in the civil rights struggle. With so many decisions to be made, I decided that I would return to Pilgrim for one year, with an eye toward college the following year. Mr. C. O. Hollis, Senior Vice President—Marketing at Pilgrim, had kept in touch with me during my military tour of duty and welcomed me back to Pilgrim. I resumed my travels for the company as a special representative in the marketing department. While I enjoyed my work at Pilgrim, I felt that there was much more for me to do, and that a college education was necessary to propel me to higher positions in the company. I began to look at various colleges and their offerings. While most of the African-Americans in my area attended the historical black colleges and universities, I explored Augusta College, a historical white college, and a part of the University System of Georgia. I discovered that Augusta College had begun to desegregate and that a few African-American students were on campus. I applied for admission and received a letter of acceptance. It never crossed my mind that I would be blazing a new trail. I simply was determined to utilize my military benefits as a veteran to further my education at the least expensive school. I was able to transfer all of the college credits that I had earned while attending college at night at Fort Hood. As an entering sophomore, I discovered that there were

31

a few other African-American students who were also entering as transfer students.

## *Augusta College*

The African-American students encountered episodes of overt racism. There was a particular professor who openly used the word "nigger" during his lectures. There were white students who refused to sit next to us in class. So determined was I to earn a degree that I simply ignored the racist instances. Although some of the African-American students complained, their voices were not heard. I led a movement for the African-American students to form an organization from which we could vent our frustrations. Following several organizational meetings, we approached the administration about organizing a Black Student Union. The president expressed some reservations about the name Black Student Union. He proposed that if we selected another name, he would support our organizing on campus. We decided that we would call ourselves the Progressive Student Alliance in order to gain a college-supported charter. After we received our charter, we amended our bylaws, and changed our name from the Progressive Student Alliance to the Black Student Union. My fellow students elected me president. As president, I had some anxious moments trying to navigate the organization to become an effective campus organization. There were some students who wanted to boycott classes in order to draw media attention to the racist atmosphere on campus. I resisted this strategy. I reasoned that with only two hundred students on campus out of a student body in excess of three thousand, boycotting classes would not make a difference.

I persuaded the organization to petition the administration for a meeting with the president. The president met with us and promised to address our concerns. Shortly afterward, the college hired its first black administrator. The college hired Dr. Roscoe Williams as assistant dean of students. Dr. Williams was an excellent choice for this sensitive position. The students respected him and he was a strong and effective voice for the students. Many of the Black students found a listening ear in

Dr. Williams. A listening ear was required during the Homecoming events of 1970. The Black Student Union sponsored a young African-American lady as a candidate for Miss Augusta College. Because the votes for the white candidates were split due to the large number of candidates, the Black Student Union's candidate received the highest number of votes. This situation presented a problem for the administration and the white student body. How could they allow a historically white college to present a black student as Miss Homecoming Queen? There were attempts to invalidate the votes. We insisted that the votes should stand as counted. Ultimately, the administration announced that the votes were invalid due to some technicalities, and that the runner-up, who was white, would be crowned as Miss Augusta College. The Black Student Union, having exhausted all channels, decided that we would stage a protest at mid-court during the halftime ceremony. Our protest was pulled off in view of the crowd in attendance as well as the local television viewing audience. Some of my fellow students urged all of the black students to withdraw from school. I took a strong stand against withdrawing and convinced a majority of our membership to remain in school. We remained in school and continued our education.

I did well in my classes. I made the dean's list and was ultimately named to "Who's Who Among Students in American Colleges and Universities." Some of our professors were strong allies and encouraged the black students not to give up under trying circumstances. One of my accounting professors, Dr. Martha Farmer, was sympathetic and would offer her assistance to me. She always offered a kind remark. Another professor, Dr. Ralph Walker, who taught political science, was the most liberal professor that I had at the college. Dr. Walker did not hesitate to express his disdain for the way the minority students were being treated. I felt an air of freedom in his class that I did not feel in my other classes. Dr. Frank Hodges was equally as supportive. Dr. Hodges, a management professor, was the first professor to encourage me to enter graduate school at the University of Georgia. Dr. Hodges had earned his doctorate from the University of Georgia and had some con-

tacts at the university. He offered to write a letter of recommendation and to support my candidacy for graduate school.

Although I did not tell my associates at Pilgrim about my
plans to continue my education, I was determined to enter
graduate school. Following my graduation from Augusta
College, I returned to Pilgrim to resume my insurance career
in management. I was given more responsibility as an assistant
regional director in marketing. I was responsible for field operations in Alabama and Western Georgia. While I thoroughly
enjoyed my work, I had a nagging urge to return to school.
After working for a year, I entered the University of Georgia in
pursuit of a masters degree. I was the only African-American
student in the graduate Risk Management program. While my
studies were challenging, I finished my masters degree in one
year. During my graduate studies, I continued to work with
Pilgrim on a part-time basis. I conducted sales training workshops on Saturdays. This employment was very much appreciated in that the income helped to support our tight budget.

Upon graduation from the University of Georgia, I
returned full time to Pilgrim. I was quite excited about resum-
ing my career. By now, I had set my sights on the top marketing position at Pilgrim. I knew that it would require a lot of
hard work and sacrifices to get to the top at Pilgrim. There
were guys I reported to who had been with the company
longer than I had, who also had their sights on the chief marketing officer's job too. In this regard, I felt some jealousy
directed toward me as I made strides toward accomplishing
my goal. I felt that my level of preparation and hard work
would pay off and that I did not have to engage in the politics
that some of my colleagues participated in.

In 1976, Pilgrim's chief marketing officer, C. O. Hollis, Sr.,
announced his retirement. The company invited those individuals who had an interest in the position to apply. I submitted
an application. I felt that I had an excellent chance at the position. My record of performance was outstanding. My level of
education was superior to that of anyone in the company's
marketing department. I was crushed when the company
announced that the position had been extended to someone
else. I pondered my next move. I was not a quitter and accept-

ed the fact that politics sometimes counts more than preparation. Many of my marketing colleagues expressed anger and disappointment that I had been passed over by someone whose record of accomplishment was not comparable to mine. I later discovered that the person who had been appointed to the position had close religious ties to one of the key board members and had apparently lobbied and influenced this person to campaign on his behalf.

The company offered me the position of second in line to the chief marketing officer, as associate marketing officer, with a very nice raise in pay. While I was disappointed in having been passed over, this position proved to be very beneficial in terms of my continued growth and development. I studied the strategies and decisions that the chief marketing officer made and weighed their effectiveness. In doing so, I was able to learn from his mistakes. His marketing program was ineffective. He was authoritative and did not seek input from the senior field managers. Some of the managers rebelled and threatened to resign. The company's growth became stagnant. Many of the field managers complained to the company's CEO, and pretty soon it was obvious that his days as the chief marketing officer were limited.

Early one Saturday morning I received a telephone call from the executive vice president, Solomon Walker II, asking me to meet with him in his home in a couple of hours. He said that the issue was sensitive and monumental. I had no idea what was on his mind. In our meeting, he said that he was disappointed with the marketing department's performance and had decided to make some changes. He offered me the position of senior vice president—chief marketing officer and a seat on the company's board of directors. I was surprised at the rapid pace at which he wanted to make the changes. Although less than three years had elapsed since I had been passed over for the position of chief marketing officer, a position that I coveted, I had learned so much more about the challenges of the position. I had learned that the person who held this position had to be a very strong individual, but one who was not afraid to engage in participatory decision-making. I now understood the gravity of the job and felt that I was fully prepared to lead the company's marketing program. The importance of the marketing division could be summed up in terms of the department generating 82 percent of the company's total income.

While I was excited about taking on this awesome responsibility, I felt sorry for the individual who was being removed. I asked Mr. Walker if he had decided on the future of the person, and whether his future was secure. Mr. Walker assured me that this person would be offered a senior position in management, but with no involvement in marketing. I was given the freedom to put a marketing team in any place of my choosing. I decided that I would not make any immediate changes. I was determined to allow the current team to remain in place and sort things out over a period of time. This decision proved to be costly. A few of the key individuals from the previous administration continued to conduct themselves in the same manner as before. In some instances, my leadership was being undermined. I quickly decided to make some changes. Finally, our efforts were paying off. We received national recognition from the National Insurance Association for our success in marketing.

My success as chief marketing officer at Pilgrim caught the attention of member companies in the National Insurance Association, who extended employment offers to me. For example, during the National Insurance Association's Convention in New Orleans, Mr. Lloyd Wheeler, President of Supreme Life Insurance Company out of Chicago, handed me his business card and asked me to call him. When I called Mr. Wheeler, he said that he had been following my career and wanted to invite my wife, Barney, and me to fly to Chicago to meet with him and Mr. John Johnson, Chairman of the Board, and the publisher of Ebony and Jet magazines. I accepted his all-expenses paid invitation and flew to Chicago. My wife and I were met at the airport by Mr. Johnson's personal chauffeur, Paul, and taken to an expensive hotel suite. I was in awe in meeting Mr. Johnson. Mr. Johnson's contributions to our country as a publisher and philanthropist were awesome. He hosted lunch for us in his private dining room at his corporate headquarters. Although I deeply admired Mr. Johnson and appreciated his employment offer as senior vice president-chief marketing officer for Supreme Life Insurance Company, I had no desire to leave Pilgrim or move to Chicago.

Shortly after I declined the offer to move to Chicago, I received an offer to move to Durham, North Carolina. I received a call from Mr. Bert Collins, President-CEO of North Carolina Mutual Life Insurance Company, inviting me to meet with him in Durham. Again, Barney and I flew to meet with another company to listen to their employment offer, asking me to assume the senior marketing officer's position. During our visit in Durham, Mr. Collins arranged for me to meet with several members of the company's senior management team, who expressed their eagerness regarding my joining them. The evening included a fabulous dinner at an exclusive private club. Although I was quite impressed with Mr. Collins and his organization, I did not think that Barney and I would be as happy in Durham. Following my visit to Durham, I received another call from an executive search firm in New York asking me to meet with them in New York for an interview. The search firm was representing an unnamed life insurance company who was seeking a chief marketing officer. I flew to New York and listened to the presentation. The executive from the search firm assured me that I would be a perfect match for the company and that they were willing to meet my financial needs. After days of considering their proposal, I declined the offer.

Although Pilgrim was enjoying success, its market share was shrinking. The shrinkage was due in large measure to a changing socio-economic environment. When Pilgrim was founded in 1898 by Solomon W. Walker, with the help of three young associates, Walter S. Hornsby, Thomas J. Hornsby, and J. C. Collier, it had the African-American market all to itself. The white companies did not market their products to African-Americans in large measures.

The winds of social change had begun to blow with Thurgood Marshall's successful challenge to school desegregation in 1954. They gained momentum during the '60s with the Reverend Martin Luther King's assault on segregation and discrimination. An unexpected consequence of these changes was

to increase competition from white-owned insurance companies for black policyholders, black employees, and black business. As changing times at the beginning of the twentieth century gave birth to Pilgrim, so changing times at the end of the
twentieth century contributed to its demise.

By the late '80s, Pilgrim was experiencing financial difficulty. The company's attempt to maintain Georgia's legal reserve
requirements was difficult. The cost of market research and
development, advertising, and new product development
introduction was too costly. Our senior management team,
Solomon W. Walker II, Walter S. Hornsby III, Clarence O.
Hollis, Jr., and myself, spent hours developing strategies to
keep Pilgrim viable. We traveled to Hartford, Connecticut to
meet with the CEO of Aetna Life Insurance Company to nego-
tiate capital infusion into Pilgrim in order to strengthen its balance sheet. We had extended negotiations with the Georgia
Department of Insurance in an attempt to ease the legal
reserve requirements. We attempted to merge with Central
Life Insurance Company out of Florida, but met with no success. All of our efforts failed.

The Georgia Department of Insurance financial examiners
rendered the final blow. The Pilgrim Health and Life Insurance
Company was declared financially impaired. This impairment
meant that Pilgrim would have to close down. We entered into
discussions with Atlanta Life Insurance Company to form
steps of acquisition of Pilgrim by Atlanta Life. Jesse Hill, Jr.,
President and CEO of Atlanta Life Insurance Company,
arranged with the Georgia Department of Insurance to acquire
Pilgrim at only a fraction of what Pilgrim was worth. Mr. Hill
indicated that he would maintain Pilgrim's operations in their
current form. He came to Augusta and met with all of the
employees in a general meeting. Following the general meeting, Mr. Hill met with some of the senior officers in one-on-one
meetings. In the meeting with me, he offered me a vice presidential position in their marketing department. Mr. Hill
assured me that the position would be fulfilling and challenging. I respectfully listened and told him that I would inform
him of my decision in due time. However, by this time I had
decided that I did not want to move from the Augusta area to

Atlanta. My roots were already established and my family was quite happy in Thomson. In this regard, I considered several opportunities with other organizations in the Augusta area for employment. Dr. Fran Tedesco, President of the Medical College of Georgia, had offered me an attractive position at the Medical College of Georgia. Dr. Richard Wallace, President of Augusta College, had called with a teaching offer in the School of Business at Augusta College. Lee Curly, Branch Manager for Robinson-Humphrey brokerage firm called and extended an employment offer as a broker with his firm. Bert Collins, President of North Carolina Mutual Life Insurance in Durham North Carolina, also extended me an offer as a senior marketing officer with North Carolina Mutual.

*Chapter Six*

# NEW CAREER

I FINALLY DECIDED ON a new career. Dr. Martha Farmer, Dean of the School of Business Administration at Augusta College, offered me an endowed chair as the Cree-Walker professor of business. As an endowed business professor, I would teach a reduced load of classes in finance and economics and serve as an ambassador to the business community. I felt good about the opportunity to return to my alma mater, and especially to become associated with a professor, Martha Farmer, who had befriended me when I was a student at the college. In those tension-filled days of desegregation and hostility on campus, Dr. Farmer was empathetic and treated all of her students with dignity and respect. While she was a demanding accounting professor who did not relax her expectations, she was extremely sensitive to the pressure that we, as black students, were experiencing. Thus, I looked forward to joining the faculty under her leadership.

It was amazing to me to see the changes at Augusta College. Twenty years had passed since I had studied there as a student. I had grown so much as a person, and the college had grown so much as an institution. My experiences in the corporate world had prepared me more than I realized to enter the classroom as a professor. My experiences in education as a policymaker also served me well. My understanding of governance and state funding were valuable tools as well.

Although I had served as a part-time professor many years earlier at Augusta College, I did not realize how fulfilling teaching at the college level would be. I quickly settled into my classes and looked forward to going to the campus everyday. I thoroughly enjoyed the intellectual stimulation from my colleagues and the challenging questions from my students. While I had spent more than thirty enjoyable years in the business world, the world of academia was totally different. I relished the idea of starting all over again.

One of my associates, Dr. Bill Dowling, Chairman of the Department of Finance and Accounting, encouraged me to collect some of the articles that I had written on financial planning and economic topics and publish them into a book. With his encouragement and the support of his administrative assistant, Deloris Wright, I began the task of writing a book. After months of work, I was able to publish *Matters of Money*. The book was well received and led to my doing financial seminars and workshops on finance and economics.

One of the great rewards of teaching is to see the difference you are making in the lives of students. In this regard, I received the highest honor that you can receive when I was awarded the Outstanding Faculty Award in 2000. One of my colleagues, Dr. Wayne Mixon, nominated me for consideration. I received letters of support from students, community leaders, and fellow colleagues. One of the most touching letters came from one of my former students, who likened my influence on him as lighting a candle in a dark room so that others could see.

## *My Special Gifts from God*

Barney and I had a great life as husband and wife. We enjoyed each other's company and supported each other in every way possible. Still, after eight years of marriage, we were not complete. We wanted a child of our own. God answered our prayers and gave us the most beautiful daughter that you could ever hope to have. On June 27, 1969, Cathy Jochelle was born at the McDuffie County Hospital. She was simply beautiful and bright and brought so much joy to our lives.

Cathy was a well-rounded person who was gifted in many respects. She played piano, did ballet dance, was an active church member where she played piano for the Sunday school, and was an excellent student who received various academic achievement awards, including the regional spelling bee contest. Cathy was a well-behaved girl who would grow up to make us so proud of her. Following her graduation as an honor student from Thomson High School, she entered the University of Georgia where she excelled as a pre-medicine candidate with a major in biology. Following her graduation from the University of Georgia, Cathy entered the Medical College of Georgia, where she earned a doctorate in research. Her post-doctoral work would take her to Cornell Medical University in New York, where she continued to excel. Cathy would later marry Tyrone Hatcher, and to this union our first grandson, Colin Zachary Hatcher, was born June 30, 1999.

Although Cathy brought so much happiness to us, Barney and I wanted another child. God answered our prayers again. On July 18, 1978, our son, Joseph David, Jr. was born at the University Hospital in Augusta. He was an active boy who was lovingly adored by us. While Cathy was pretty quiet and reserved, David was just the opposite. He was affable and made friends easily. He tended to socialize much more than Cathy, which in some instances took his mind off his studies. Although intellectually gifted, David was not nearly as serious about his studies. He played varsity football and played in the school band. Following David's graduation from Thomson High School, he entered Savannah State University. He later transferred to Paine College and eventually dropped out of college.

While a student at Paine College, David met our future daughter-in-law, Mistey P. Harris. David and Mistey married, and to this union our second grandson was born, Joseph David Greene, III on September 4, 2002.

## *My Bout with Cancer*

Although I had lived with the threat of cancer most of my life, I did not know that my day would come so soon with a different form of cancer. My father of from colon cancer at age fifty. Most of his sisters and brothers also died of colon cancer. My sister, Christine, died of colon cancer at the young age of forty. Most of my relatives on my father's side of the family were cancer victims. Following my sister's death in 1982, I was diagnosed with precancerous polyps, which required extensive surgery resulting in most of my large intestines being removed. After my recovery from surgery, I began a systematic annual screening program for colon cancer. These annual exams always brought about a degree of anxiety. Would the lab results be positive or negative? Although there were moments of anxiety, there was no fear. I had long outlived any fear of cancer or death. My faith in God gave me a certain assurance and peace of mind. I always felt that I would be affected in some way by colon cancer.

Much to my surprise, I was diagnosed with lymphoma cancer of the neck in 1998. My wife, Barney, noticed that I had a small swollen area under my left jaw, which led to the diagnosis. Surgery was performed on July 6, 1998, at the Medical College of Georgia. I could see the deep concern in Barney's eyes as they prepared me for surgery. My pastor, Reverend F. D. Favors, joined us in the preparation room and offered prayer for me. He remained at Barney's side for the duration of the surgery, and until I was removed from the recovery room.

Barney was a pillar of strength for me. She did all in her power to support me during the months of treatment. The chemotherapy treatment was grueling. I felt weak and tired most of the time. Although I did not have a taste for food, I forced myself to eat. While I did not have an appetite, I could tolerate tuna salads relatively well. As a result, I had tuna almost daily. During this most difficult time in my life, I gained renewed appreciation for friends and loved ones. The telephone calls, letters, and cards poured in daily. While I continued to work, my colleagues at Augusta State University were supportive. Some of the professors offered to do some of my lectures, and my dean suggested that I take time off. Although there were days when I was so weak that I could barely walk steadily, I did not take a single day off. With God's help, I made it through a most miserable time in my life.

Following months of treatment of chemotherapy and radiation, I was declared cured. However, I would remain under close scrutiny and medical observation for the next five years.

The oncology team at the Medical College were caring professionals who provided me with excellent care during my treat-
ments. As a cancer survivor, I resolved to become a volunteer
advocate for the American Cancer Society. In this role, I delivered speeches at various Relay For Life Cancer functions for
the organization. I delivered speeches in Augusta, Beaufort,
South Carolina, Thomson, and Harlem, Georgia. I joined the
Georgia American Cancer Society delegation for a trip to our
nation's capitol to promote national support for research and
treatment for cancer patients. In Washington, I spoke to senators and representatives and urged them to support our cause.
In speaking with Senator Edward Kennedy, I was encouraged
by his comments of support. He said that he was sensitive to
our cause and would continue to support more money for
research and treatment.

The American Cancer Society's Relay For Life has become
a very special annual event in Thomson. Many of the key supporters are cancer survivors, including our Mayor, Robert E.
Knox, Jr. The Relay For Life event in Thomson is held at
Thomson High School's track field. Hundreds of people gather for an all-night event. Community organizations, including
churches, set up tents and provide food in a festival atmosphere. People share survival stories and extend greetings and
support to others who are fighting cancer. One of the objec-
tives is to attract monetary support for the American Cancer
Society. In this regard, I have raised several thousands of dollars by soliciting contributions from family and friends.

Emanuel County
High School (1957)

Our wedding

Who's Who
Augusta College
(1971)

Promotion
(U.S. Army)

Army Life

**ELECT**

# JOSEPH D. GREENE

–ELECT–

# Joseph D. Greene

Member
McDuffie County Board
of Education

Georgia School Boards Association (December 17, 1981)

State Health
Planning Board

Board of Regents (January 11, 1984)

Oath of Office (Governor's Office), 1982

Oath of Office (Board of Regents)

Pilgrim Board
of Directors

Healthcare Georgia

First Bank Board of Directors

Economics Lecture—Augusta State University (2000)

# CHAIRMAN'S
## LETTER

The Honorable Joe Frank Harris
Office of the Governor
203 State Capitol
Atlanta, Georgia 30334

Dear Governor Harris:

On behalf of the Board of Regents, I offer the annual report for the University System of Georgia for the fiscal year July 1, 1988 through June 30, 1989.

In the past several years, we have made great progress in the University System. This year signified, I think, a continuation of our efforts to reach some important goals we have set for Georgia's 34 public colleges and universities. Collectively, these efforts and the events that unfolded in the past 12 months point to a distinguishing characteristic of our System. That characteristic is momentum.

One piece of evidence of our momentum lies in our continued success in making higher education accessible to as many Georgians as possible. Fall quarter 1988 began a new era of entrance requirements -- requirements designed to improve the caliber of our students and the quality of our instruction. Despite these tougher requirements, fall quarter enrollment figures rose 5.2 percent, a sure sign that our institutions remain accessible to the state's citizens.

Another progressive step contributing to increased educational opportunities in the state was made with the approval of a new institution classification, "regional university." As these institutions are created, regional areas of the state will enjoy tremendous benefits. My colleagues on the Board and I agree that with regional universities, we can increase opportunities for economic, social and cultural development.

Education has long been known as the great equalizer. This year the System took a monumental leap -- one of the most important to date -- toward equalizing higher education in Georgia. A committee of college presidents, academic officers and System staff members conducted a study to examine how to get more minorities, both students and faculty, involved in the state's public higher education institutions.

Governor, the thorough efforts of this committee are to be applauded. I believe the recommendations outlined in this important document represent a new hope for the state's minority population. Thus, it is with great conviction that I say we must do everything in our power to act upon the tenets of the report -- that we turn these fine suggestions into action and, in doing so, pledge a new commitment to those who traditionally have not benefited from our services as they should have.

Great strides have been made in Georgia's public higher education, but there remains much work to be done. Many resources keep the momentum of success building, but the University System's most important asset is people. Without them, we could accomplish nothing.

I extend thanks to the many people who contribute to the successes the University System has enjoyed. The people who keep our institutions running -- faculty, staff and students -- deserve our sincere gratitude.

My personal appreciation goes to you, the members of the General Assembly, and the people of Georgia for the continuous and generous support you've given public higher education. I am equally grateful to the Chancellor, his staff, and the members of the Student Advisory Council for their contributions. Finally, I also extend special thanks to the other members of the Board for their dedication and commitment to the goals toward which we all strive.

Sincerely,

Joseph D. Greene
Chairman, Board of Regents

# Passing the Gavel

*Vice Chairman Joseph Greene is elected to the Board's top spot for 1988-89.*

*Newly elected chairman Joseph Greene: Diligent, diplomatic.*

If the June meeting is any indication, next year's Board of Regents will be led by a man whom others will enthusiastically support.

Evidence of that assertion was prominent at the June 8 session, which brought the election of Joseph Greene, an insurance executive from Thomson, Georgia and this year's vice chairman of the Board, to the chairmanship for the 1988-89 year. Family and friends were on hand to lend him moral support. His fellow Regents voted unanimously to elect him to the post. Finally, his colleagues and members of the central office staff endorsed him through a round of applause.

For Greene, 47, being elected chairman is the latest in a lifetime of accomplishments. He joined the Pilgrim Health and Life Insurance Company in 1959 as a salesman, and over the years he worked his way up to executive vice president and chief marketing officer. In 1971, he became the first black elected official in McDuffie County when voted to the county school board, a post he held for the next 13 years. In 1984, he gave up the seat when Gov. Joe Frank Harris named him to the Board of Regents as an at-large member.

It was Greene's diligence and diplomatic approach to matters that contributed to his being named vice chairman last year. Such fortune and opportunity, however, have not always come easily in his lifetime. "Graduating from a segregated high school 30 years ago, there were only three public colleges in Georgia open to me because of my color," Greene said in his remarks to the Board. "And these three were closed [to me] because I did not have the money to attend them."

Throughout his professional career, Greene has remained dedicated to worthwhile causes in the Thomson and Augusta communities. He is active in a number of philanthropic organizations — Red Cross, United Way, Easter Seal Society, to name a few — as well as civic organizations such as Civic Club, Rotary Club and Boy Scouts. **S**

## The New VC

*Vice Chairman Edgar Rhodes*

Those who know Regent Edgar Rhodes know that though he speaks softly and deliberately, his words carry great weight, sincerity and, occasionally, humor. For that, his colleagues on the Board appreciate him. And when they unanimously elected him vice chairman for next year, he thanked them with characteristic humility.

"It pleases me to no end that you would ask me to serve as vice chairman," Rhodes told his fellow Regents. "I had no idea when I joined this Board that you would someday consider me for this position."

Rhodes, a vice president of the City Lumber Company in Bremen, Georgia, has chaired the Board's education committee since the departure this year of Regent Marie Dodd. He is a consummate activist in his community, serving on such organizations as the Bremen City Council, Bremen School Board and the First National Bank of Haralson County. He is also a charter member of the local Rotary Club and belongs to the area hospital authority.

Rhodes was sworn in to the Board early in 1985 as a representative of the sixth district. He is a graduate of the University of Georgia, where he earned a B.S.A. degree in 1938. But despite his years of experience in business and community, he may be in for some new experiences as a leader on the Board. After Rhodes was elected vice chairman, Board Chair Jackie Ward told him, "Edgar, I offer you my sincere condolences."

*Chapter Seven*

# BOARDS AND COMMISSIONS

I LEARNED EARLY IN life that the best way to effect change is from the inside. No matter how loud the voice, it is seldom heard in the boardroom unless you are sitting around the table as a member where decisions are made. Evidence of this can best be explained by an experience I had while serving on the McDuffie County Selective Service Draft Board.

## *McDuffie County Selective Service Draft Board (1969–1972)*

President Lyndon Johnson issued a mandate that required all of the nation's Selective Service draft boards to recruit minority board members. The McDuffie County Selective Service Draft Board was an all-white board. The irony of the composition of the board was that more than half of the young men who were drafted to serve in the United States Army were young black men. This was not unique in our county. The ethnic profile of the boards throughout the south was similar, all white. Mr. Eulie B. Johnson, a veteran of World War II, and I were selected to become the first African-Americans to serve on the McDuffie County Selective Service board.

I was amazed to learn that a disproportionate percentage of the young white men were granted deferrals. In one instance, there was a young African-American man who

requested conscientious objection status, in opposition to the
Vietnam War. He was in college, and requested some form of
civil service in lieu of military induction. The chairman of the
board, blurted, "Draft him; he cannot tell us where he wants to
serve." I listened intently as the other members of the board
uttered similar comments. Finally, I spoke up and said, "Mr.
Chairman, is it fair for us to draft this young black man who
has asked us to assign him to some form of civil service, while
not taking any action whatsoever against the young white man
who wrote us an obscene letter last month, and told us to go to
hell, and this board, to my dismay concluded that he would
not make a good soldier and left him alone?" In response to
my comments, one of the board members commented, "Well,
Joseph has a point here. Let us give this boy a deferment." I
have often reflected on that experience, and concluded that if I
had not been on the inside of that board, an injustice would
have been committed to a young man who offered himself for
service to our country.

An intense experience occurred when the military prose-
cuted Lt. William Calley for crimes committed in Vietnam. He
was charged with leading his platoon into killing innocent
women and children during a military sweep in My Lai, a
Vietnamese village. His conviction created quite a controversy
throughout the south. Many draft board members resigned in
protest. The chairman of our board called me to inform me that
he and the other white members were resigning, and said to
me, "I am sure you will go along with our decision." I
responded by saying that I would not resign, because I felt that
Lt. Calley's conviction was justified. Having just returned from
my military tour of duty, I reminded the chairman that we
were taught how to conduct ourselves, and that in my opinion,
Lt. Calley did not conduct himself properly in firing on those
innocent women and children. I called Mr. Johnson, a black
board member, to share with him the discussion that I had
with the chairman of our board, and of my decision not to
resign. When the news broke that I had not resigned from the
draft board, I began receiving threatening phone calls. My life
was threatened and I was told to watch my back. My friend E.
G. Long offered to come to my home and to set up a security

watch for the safety of my family. After a few days, the threatening telephone calls stopped.

Mr. Johnson and I were the lone members of the McDuffie County Selective Service Draft Board for ten days. After ten days, the chairman of the board announced that he and the other members of the draft board who had resigned were returning as board members.

## *Ten-Sixties Advisory Board (1969–1973)*

In response to racial polarization that was occurring in many small southern communities as they desegregated schools and public facilities, the Thomson business community leaders formed an advisory board to promote racial harmony. The Ten-Sixties organization was in effect, a chamber of commerce. The stated goal was to create a climate in Thomson that would attract industry and create jobs. The Ten-Sixties organization, in establishing an advisory arm, did not elect to call the advisory body a biracial committee as most communities did. However, the substance of our work was that of a biracial committee.

The advisory board was made up of an equal number of black and white citizens, whom the parent organization felt were citizens who wanted to promote racial harmony. Although in some instances our discussions were heated and candid, we were able to put our personal feelings and prejudices aside and reach an accord. We were able to agree on approaches that we collectively felt would be in the community's best interest. Through this organization, we were able to diffuse situations that could have polarized the community along racial lines.

We made recommendations to the various governmental agencies in terms of equal employment opportunities, housing, education, and law enforcement. I attribute much of Thomson's image as a progressive community to the work that the advisory board did behind the scenes. While we often fought among ourselves during our deliberations, we were able to present a united front to the community. As a result of our work as a biracial group, we demonstrated that people of different ethnic backgrounds could work in a spirit of harmony for the good of their community. I left this board after four years of work with a different appreciation and perspective on the commonality of humanity.

## United Way of Thomson McDuffie (1977–1979)

When I was asked' to accept a seat on the United Way board, I did not hesitate. The United Way's mission of helping community organizations and agencies to enhance the quality of life of the citizenry appealed to me. After one year on the board, I was elected as president of the United Way. My election as president made history in that I became the first African-American to hold this position. The position afforded me the opportunity to use the influence of the presidency to fund some of the smaller, less-known community-based organizations that had been denied participation in the past. For example, we funded the RSC Club for the first time. The RSC Club was an arm of a minority civic club. The RSC Club provided recreational activities for the black youth in the community, including operating a large swimming pool. My being in the right position on the inside of an organization made a positive difference for our community.

## Metro-Augusta Chamber of Commerce
## (1989–1992)

A call came into me from the chairman of the Metro-Augusta Chamber of Commerce nominating committee asking me to serve on their board of directors. I reminded the caller that while I worked in Augusta, I did not reside in Augusta and suggested that I probably would not be the appropriate candidate. He responded by saying that the committee was aware of my residence and that it was of no concern to them. I reluctantly accepted the chamber's invitation to serve. At my first board meeting, I discovered that of eighteen board members, they had only one African-American member, Dr. Julius Scott, President of Paine College. Dr. Scott was the first person to welcome me to the board and expressed his delight in having another minority member on the chamber board. I found the work with the chamber very gratifying in that we were able to provide leadership in promoting economic growth in our service area.

## *Pilgrim Health and Life Insurance Company (1979–1990)*

As I walked the corridor at Pilgrim's corporate office, I often looked at the bronze plaque on the wall bearing the likeness of the company's founders. I admired the men who, barely out of slavery, founded the company. To think that I would become a member of the company's board of directors and sit in the boardroom where the founders' portraits also hung on the walls was a humbling experience. As the newly appointed senior vice president and chief marketing officer, I was elected to the company's board of directors by the company's stockholders. Our meetings always started with an extended devotion, led by Dr. Charles Butler, a retired educator. Dr. Butler was quite a philosopher and orator. He would captivate the board with his Shakespearean discourse on wisdom and life.

Pilgrim's board was a divided board. The board was divided along family lines between the Hornsbys and the Walkers. A family rift had developed long before I came to Pilgrim. The basis of the division was born out of a fight for control and leadership of the company. S. W. Walker, a grocery delivery boy, founded the company in 1898. Mr. Walker was supported by his cousin, W. S. Hornsby, and other relatives. The company thrived harmoniously during its stage of infancy. However, following the death of S. W. Walker, the founder, W. S. Hornsby became president of the company. Following Mr. Hornsby's death there was a power struggle for control of the company. Mr. W. S. Hornsby, Jr., son of the elder Hornsby, emerged as president, which created division between the Hornsbys and Walkers. Their grandsons, S. W. Walker II, and W. S. Hornsby III, were my contemporaries. Both of them graduated from Morehouse College and followed in their father's footsteps in working for Pilgrim. The grandsons, S. W. Walker II and W. S. Hornsby III, were well educated and committed to Pilgrim. Each one had his followers within the company and always seemed to be in competition with each other. The company's organization chart also was organized along the respective grandsons' line of authority. That is, roughly one half of the company's departments reported to each grandson. My department, marketing, reported to S. W. Walker II. Our board also reflected the family division. The Hornsby family had a board seat for a granddaughter, Willenia Butler, and the Walker family seat was held by granddaughter Dorothy Pleasant.

There was a movement to restructure the company and replace Mr. W. S. Hornsby, Jr. as president. Tensions were extremely high at the board meeting as the restructuring committee recommended the removal of Mr. Hornsby. Tempers flared and emotions were high as Mr. Hornsby was removed as president. S. W. Walker II was named chairman and chief executive officer, and W. S. Hornsby III was named president. The bitterness between the two families was so obvious and painful. I often reflected on the toll that the division had on the company.

As the company's market share continued to shrink, the company's board of directors fought off an attempt by the Booker T. Washington Life Insurance Company, of Birmingham, Alabama, to acquire Pilgrim. We also made overtures to Central Life Insurance Company, based in Florida, to effect a friendly merger. Our efforts were futile.

As a board, we struggled to keep Pilgrim afloat in the midst of external forces that were beyond our control. Pilgrim had suffered from the lack of strategic visionary planning, and it became apparent to me that our days as a viable company were numbered.

## National Insurance Association (1987–1989)

The National Insurance Association was a trade association of the black-owned insurance companies in the United States, headquartered in Chicago, Illinois. The association conducted executive development programs, sales institutes, marketing strategies, and annual promotional programs. The association had two divisions within the organization. There was a home office section and a marketing section. One of the most rewarding educational experiences that I've had occurred when I attended the National Insurance Association's management development institute in 1965 at Dillard University.

I became active in the association, doing workshop presentations and speeches. My visibility in the association led to my election as vice president of the marketing division of the association and a seat on the national board of directors. One of the values of the office was the establishment of lifelong friendships from officers of member companies of the association.

## State Health Planning Board (1979–1983)

I received a letter from Governor Joe Frank Harris informing me that he wanted to appoint me to the State Health Planning Board. The State Health Planning Board played an important role in determining the accessibility of healthcare facilities in Georgia. The board had the responsibility of issuing certificates of needs to facilities such as hospitals and nursing homes, while being careful to avoid overlapping services. I found the work on the board very interesting and challenging. The work was not without controversy. For example, there was a delegation of black citizens from Hancock County who filed for a certificate of needs to establish a new hospital in Sparta, Georgia. As we considered the application, there was a group of white citizens who filed a petition in opposition to our granting approval. We conducted hearings from both sides of the issue. The board determined, through the hearings, that what seemed to be an issue of access to health care in the area really was an issue of control. That is, the white citizens who filed the opposing petition did not want the black citizens to operate the facility in Hancock County. For instance, the county and city governmental officials had experienced racial tension as the black citizens gained more influence by electing more African-Americans to various offices in the county. We approved the certificate of needs and for the first time in decades, the citizens of Hancock County had their own hospital.

## Morris Museum Board of Directors
### (1996–2002)

During my years of public service, it was normal for me to receive telephone calls from the media requesting my views and comments on various topics. However, I was surprised to receive a telephone call from William S. Morris, publisher of the *Augusta Chronicle* newspaper. Mr. Morris normally delegated inquiry calls to members of his staff. The purpose of his call was different. He called to invite me to accept a seat on the Morris Museum Board of Directors. He commented about my range of experience as a former regent, and the fact that he was concerned about more diversity on the board. I responded by saying that my schedule was pretty full and that I could not give a lot of time to this project. Mr. Morris assured me that if I accepted his invitation, that my responsibility as a board member would not become too cumbersome, and that all of the board members were extremely busy people.

I found the work on the Morris Museum Board quite gratifying and culturally enriching. During my tenure on the board, I was able to establish friendships with people whom I would not normally come in contact with. For instance, I often engaged in lengthy conversations with retired Air Force General Perry Smith, a noted national commentator on military affairs with national news outlets, on defense issues.

## Southeastern Technology Board of Directors
### (1996–2002)

I have never touted myself as a person who enjoys the novelty of new gadgets and technology. Thus, when I was asked to serve on the Southeastern Technology Board, I immediately assumed that the organization was deeply involved in science and technology. To the contrary, the mission was to collaborate with the Savannah River Site Nuclear Facility and other scientific engines in the community to expand the community's economic base. Our work was very interesting and beneficial. Through our efforts, we were able to create an incubator system for small start-up companies so that they could enjoy the benefits of government contracts. We were able to extend technical services and other economic resources. As a result of our efforts, several small businesses were launched and became viable entities.

## National Science Center Discovery Board of Directors (1996– )

I was asked to join the inaugural organizing board to launch the National Science Center. I readily agreed to serve on this board because of its emphasis on education in the areas of science and mathematics. The focus is to share resources with area school systems and complement their program in science and math.

The breadth of the board was impressive. Area colleges and universities were represented by their respective presidents in the board's composition. Additionally, several large national firms were represented by their presidents, as well as several high-ranking retired military officers. Our mission was to collaborate with Fort Gordon and the state Department of Education in improving the quality of education.

Through the collective effort of several national and state entities, we have been able to attract millions of dollars to Augusta to support school systems. Many of the programs that are offered are cutting-edge technology concepts where students can enjoy interactive experiences in space travel and other programs.

## Chapter Eight

# McDuffie County Board of Education (1971–1984)

HAVING BEEN ELECTED TO the McDuffie County Board of Education in 1970 was a milestone in itself. My election made history in that I became the first African-American to be elected to public office in McDuffie County. I understood the gravity of the office, and I was very serious about the office and the incumbent responsibility of a public officeholder. I also understood that, as the first minority elected to public office in the county, much more was expected of me. I always prayed to God for wisdom, understanding, and strength to do what was right in the sight of God. I knew that, while a lot of my supporters would push their own agendas, I had to march by my own will ... as revealed to me by God.

There were many controversial issues I had to grapple with. Many of the issues had racial overtones relative to personnel issues and students' rights. Although many of the problems were racially based, I always sought solutions that were humanistically based. That is, I tried to address the problems in the context of fairness, equity, and reasonableness. My attempts to mediate, to diffuse, and to heal old wounds were often misunderstood by some of my supporters. For instance, I did not attempt to embarrass my fellow board members in public by delivering a tirade about inequities in front of the media. My approach was one of quiet diplomacy ... compromise and accord in order to effect a win-win solution, when possible, for the aggrieved parties.

For example, Superintendent J. A. Maxwell was pretty inflexible and rather set in his ways. I sensed early in my tenure on the board that he would have his way on most issues. His ways were molded by more than twenty years of experience, from a conservative view, and from a segregated era.

To challenge his views in public was an exercise in futility. I felt that, while a large percentage of citizens would applaud my futile challenges, the effective approach was to study Superintendent Maxwell's tendencies and take advantage of any openings. In studying him and his views, I discovered that in a one-on-one setting, out of the public's eye, he could be very accommodating. For instance, some of our African-American teachers who lived in McDuffie County were barred from teaching in McDuffie County because they taught in a neighboring county. The reasons were varied—from a lack of vacancies when they applied to personality conflicts. I approached Mr. Maxwell on this issue. Armed with statistics, economic benefits, and the absurdity of this policy, he and I had an extended meeting in his office. He stated that the policy was born out of a "gentleman's agreement" between the local superintendents. He conceded, at my relentless urging, that the policy "probably should be reviewed." At our next board meeting, he announced to the board that he was rescinding a long-held policy on employing teachers from adjoining counties and that teachers would be considered based on qualifications. He never mentioned the private meeting that he and I had in his office. Although he received the credit for this "progressive move," in my heart I received the personal satisfaction of knowing that I had played a role in changing a policy that was wrong.

There were many problems that were resolved behind closed doors. There were times when cooler heads had to reconcile their differences and work for the common good of the school system. I learned a lot about negotiating, compromising, diplomacy, and trying to effect a win-win situation. The bottom line is, no one wants to lose.

My thirteen-year tenure on the school board was rewarding, in that through my urging we were one of the first rural school systems in Georgia to implement a public kindergarten program. Again, I had to work hard behind the scenes to convince the superintendent that an investment in early childhood development would pay off down the road. I developed an economic model on the cost-effectiveness of kindergarten.

Through my urging, we were able to demonstrate that this investment would pay off in the future. Through my urging, we were able to take advantage of the tax code, which permitted local school systems to fund their own worker's compensation program in lieu of participating in the state insurance program. We were able to develop a self-insurance program for our employees that saved our taxpayers thousand of dollars. It was not an easy sale. I had to prove its effectiveness by developing a cost-effective model through a self-funding mechanism. As a result, we were able to amass a large reserve and pay all claims.

My devotion to the McDuffie County school system caught the attention of the Georgia School Boards Association in Atlanta. The Georgia School Boards Association, made up of public school board members from Georgia's 159 counties, provided resources for school systems. The association conducted workshops on governance, education policies, and federal and state laws. I found myself appearing on panels, participating in workshops, and doing speeches for the Association. This experience led to my election to the Georgia School Boards Association Board of Directors as a district director. As a director, I was able to affect programs and policies for the state of Georgia. Meanwhile, back in Thomson, my fellow board members elected me vice chairman of the board of education for the McDuffie County School System.

My service as a director of the Georgia School Boards Association caught the attention of Governor Joe Frank Harris. Governor Harris was concerned about education reform and was determined to make drastic changes in Georgia's public education. He appointed me to the Governor's Education

Review Commission. This blue-ribbon commission was charged with developing the framework for a quality basic education in Georgia. We were commissioned for eighteen months. This was a most rewarding experience. The commission was made up of forty citizens, most of whom were well-known state leaders in business and/or public life. There were several legislators from the House and Senate who served on the commission as well. With Georgia near the bottom in education, in terms of funding, test scores, graduation rates, and other key indices, Governor Harris's Education Commission had a formidable task.

We held hearings, seeking input from education experts as well as laypeople. The work was arduous, but quite gratifying. The legislature accepted our work and passed Georgia's Quality Basic Act in 1984.

## *Board of Regents (1984–1991)*

My wife and I were en route to the Bahamas in December 1983 for a mini-vacation … when the governor's call came. Our daughter, Cathy, tried to reach us at the airport in Atlanta, but failed. She wanted to inform me that I had received an urgent call from Governor Joe Frank Harris. When I returned the governor's call to one of his senior administrative assistants, Gracie Phillips, I was told that the governor wanted to see me right away. I inquired as to the nature of his wanting to see me, but got nothing from Mrs. Phillips. She said that it was a confidential matter. I pretty much assumed that the governor wanted to discuss the Education Commission's work. Thus, in preparation for my meeting with the governor, I reviewed my notes from the commission work along with some of the issues that had been difficult to resolve, and thought through my own assessment on our progress.

When I arrived at the state capital on December 27, 1983, the governor's chief of staff, Tom Perdue, and administrative assistant Gracie Phillips met me. The meeting took place in Gracie's office as follows:

Gracie: "Tell us about your experience as a member of the McDuffie County Board of Education."

"How long have you served?"

"Your greatest rewards?"

"Give us an assessment of the Governor's Education Review Commission."

I thought to myself, as I prepared to respond, "Uh-huh, that's why I am here."

Next question from Gracie: "Would you be willing to resign from the McDuffie County Board of Education if the governor appointed you to a much higher position?"

My response: "What does the governor have in mind?"

Tom Perdue: "The governor feels that you're qualified to serve in any position in his administration ... Where would you like to serve?"

I responded by saying, "Well, I suppose in the area of education or minority business development."

Still no clue! Gracie announced that the governor wanted to see me alone.

I was taken to Governor Harris' office. We exchanged greetings, and the governor started by saying, "Thank you for coming to see me. All of the references that I have checked on you from around the state say that you are the kind of person I want in my administration. The reports that I have from the commission are that you do your homework and that you are very knowledgeable about education in Georgia. I also know that you are a hard worker, who started at the bottom in your career and has risen to the top, and that you worked and completed your education after a tour of military service for our country. You worked your way through college ... that's commendable.

"Now, let me tell you what I have in mind ... I have you in mind for an appointment to the Board of Regents; this is a seven-year term. This is the most prestigious appointment that I will make. A lot of people want this appointment ... and I am considering several. At any rate, if you're not selected for the Regents, I want you to serve somewhere else in my administration."

I expressed my deep appreciation to the governor and my sense of honor for being under consideration.

The governor then wanted me to tell him about my family and my church.

He led a conversation about his disdain for corruption in politics—about sheriffs who had been removed from office, as well as mayors for unethical and illegal conduct.

The governor thanked me and said, "You'll hear from me shortly."

Within a few days, the governor phoned me at my office at Pilgrim to inform me that I was his choice to become the newest regent. I was excited and shared the news with my secretary.

I went on to share the news with relatives and friends as we made plans to travel to Atlanta for the swearing-in ceremony. The swearing-in ceremony was scheduled for January 10, 1984 at 10:30 a.m. at the State Capitol. My favorite uncle, James Green, several cousins, my mother-in-law, and others all converged in Thomson for the drive to Atlanta. My wife, Barney, was up early that morning getting David ready for the trip to Atlanta. David and Cathy were excited as we made plans for the drive to Atlanta.

The exhilaration that I felt was simply too much to verbalize. The joy expressed by many people who had always believed in me, and their coming to the state capital for the ceremony, was a dramatic expression of their love. Their "Joseph" was where they wanted him to be. The entourage included my wife and our children, Cathy and David, my mother-in-law, Myrtle Robinson, Uncle James, Bernard Robinson, Gladys Robinson, cousins Adele Harrison, Elvira and Pete Jackson, Elizabeth Harrison, my brother, Solomon, friends Eddie Long, Ephraim Petett, Sol Walker, and Leon Booker, brother-in-law Jay Grady, and others. I thought of all of those teachers who worked so hard with a labor of love in molding my mind at the Cross-Green school and at Emanuel County High. Although the day was dismal, weather-wise (rain), my heart burned with rays of sunshine and hope; I felt numb and anxious.

## Georgia Post Secondary Board of Directors (1984–1985)

Governor Joe Frank Harris decided to overhaul the Department of Secondary Vocational Education. He was determined to make the department more efficient and to create a seamless education system in Georgia. Governor Harris wanted the various state education agencies to work more cooperatively and to share resources where feasible. In this regard, he appointed a board to oversee this process. The members of the board were pulled from Georgia's three major education departments, the Board of Regents, Adult Vocational Education, and the State Board of Education.

Governor Harris asked three regents to serve as representatives from the Board of Regents. Regent John Henry Anderson, Edgar Rhodes, and I were appointed to serve. As we commenced our work, there was a degree of tension among the members of the board. I sensed that some members were more concerned with protecting their turf than improving the quality of post secondary education. However, after months of working, we were able to make substantial progress. A major step was when the board appointed Dr. Kenneth Breeden as the new executive director of the newly formed Adult Technical Education program. His experience in vocational education was well respected and used as a catalyst toward progress.

As my term came to an end on this board, I felt that we had served the citizens of Georgia well and that the future of post secondary vocational education had been improved.

*Chapter Nine*

# BLUE CROSS/BLUE SHIELD OF GEORGIA BOARD OF DIRECTORS (1993–2001)

UPON RETURNING HOME FROM out of town my daughter, Cathy, told me that a Mr. Richard Shirk from Atlanta had called and said that it was important for me to return his call. The name was not familiar to me, so I could not imagine the nature of the call. When I reached Mr. Shirk on the telephone, he informed me that Blue Cross/Blue Shield of Georgia was interested in discussing the possibility of my becoming a member of the company's board of directors. I agreed to meet with him in Thomson over breakfast at White Columns restaurant at the Best Western Motel. He shared with me the company's mission and its focus on healthcare issues in Georgia and said that he felt that with my background in insurance, I could be of enormous value in the governance of his company. I asked Mr. Shirk to give me a few days to think about the invitation.

During the next few days, I did some research on Blue Cross/Blue Shield of Georgia and was very much impressed with the company's history of service in Georgia. I also considered the state of healthcare in our country, and the evolution of healthcare from a system of indemnification to managed-care.

65

That is, the first modern HMOs were formed by them in the late 1970s, which was a market-driven response to employers' growing concerns about the swift rise of medical benefits costs. Weighing these facts as they were presented to me, I accepted the offer from Blue Cross/Blue Shield to become a member of their board of directors.

My becoming a member of this corporate board meant that I would join a large corporate board, with eighteen members on the board. It also meant that I would become only the second African-American invited to serve on Blue Cross/Blue Shield's board. At my first board meeting at the corporate headquarters in Atlanta, Dr. Leroy Keith, President of Morehouse College, said to me: "I am delighted that you have been added to this board; now there are two of us." I quickly discovered that the board's composition was made up of highly successful business leaders from throughout Georgia. For example, there were successful bank presidents in James Laboon, President of Athens First Bank & Trust; Fred Tolbert, former President of Albany Federal Savings & Loan; James Lientz, President, Mid-South Banking Group, NationsBank, N.A.; Julia Mitchell-Ivey, former executive with First Union National Bank, Atlanta; Jerry Vereen, President and CEO of Riverside Manufacturing Company of Moultrie, Georgia; Betsy Camp, President of Camp Oil Company—a large petroleum company—who was young and extremely talented; as was Frank Hanna III, CEO of HBR Capital, Ltd. of Atlanta.

Richard Shirk, President-CEO of the company was one of the most talented business leaders that I have met. His command for details was astonishing. Dick could grasp the big picture, yet not miss the small details of the picture. His management team was equally qualified. Most of them had enjoyed success at other companies and were recruited by Dick after he joined Blue Cross/Blue Shield. To observe them managing the affairs of the company was a textbook study on how to manage a company.

Blue Cross/Blue Shield of Georgia was Georgia's largest health insurer. The company had been experiencing mediocre performance prior to Dick's arrival as president in 1992. Shortly after he assumed the leadership of the company, the company's profitability and market share began to accelerate. However, early in 1995 we started making plans to convert the company from a nonprofit company to a for-profit company. Senior management convinced the board that if we were to remain competitive, it would require an enormous infusion of capital. The best approach in raising the capital was for the company to go public with classes of stock being offered to investors. The conversion would have to be approved by Georgia's Department of Insurance and Commissioner John Oxendine. Dick and his senior management team did an outstanding job in convincing the insurance department of the merits of the conversion. With the insurance department's approval, we prepared to offer shares to investors. In this regard, one of our board members, Frank Hanna, bought a large share of the company's class of stock, worth several millions of dollars. Frank was young, intelligent, and rich. He had a keen business sense and knew a good deal when he saw one. A couple of years after the conversion, Blue Cross/Blue Shield attracted suitors. As a board, we had a fiduciary responsibility to weigh all offers in terms of protecting the stockholders' investment. We would have been derelict in not assessing acquisition proposals.

Among the offers that we reviewed was an offer from Wellpoint Insurance Company. Wellpoint was a California-based company with a huge amount of cash. Following months of negotiations, a deal was struck in 1998 to merge Blue Cross/Blue Shield of Georgia with Wellpoint Health Networks in a transaction valued at $500 million. Trigon Healthcare, Inc. made an unsolicited offer to merge with Blue Cross/Blue Shield at $675 million. Wellpoint then extended a counteroffer at $700 million. We accepted the counter offer from Wellpoint, wherein each member-shareholder of Blue Cross/Blue Shield would receive an attractive offer in excess of $5,000 per share.

In terms of governance, Wellpoint offered each member of the Blue Cross/Blue Shield Board an advisory board seat following the merger, or a substantial cash payment to resign. Many of the board members felt that Wellpoint's management style was not consistent with the historical manner in which

Blue Cross/Blue Shield had operated, and that the policyholders would not receive the same level of service. We all opted to
resign from Wellpoint.

## CSRA Community Foundation
## Board of Directors (1999– )

I received a telephone call from United States
Congressman Doug Barnard asking me to join him for lunch at
the Pinnacle Club in Augusta. Over lunch, I was invited to join
Congressman Barnard and a few other community leaders to
establish a Community Foundation. The purpose was noble in
serving as a conduit for charitable causes. Through the foundation, millions of dollars could find their way to support
charitable causes throughout the Central Savannah River Area
through various forms of philanthropy. The organization
would achieve a win-win situation for donors as well as recip-
ients. Donors would have an opportunity to establish various
tax-deductible trust arrangements where the corpus would be
protected for future disposition. The corpus's earnings would
be available for various charities.

I accepted the invitation to join the board of directors. The
foundation has made an enormous impact in a relatively short
period of time. We have been able to amass millions of dollars
in the corpus while also awarding millions to charitable organizations. Through the efforts of the CSRA Community
Foundation, small struggling organizations have been able to
remain viable and continue their missionary work of helping
people who cannot help themselves.

## Saint Joseph Hospital Board of Directors
## (2002– )

Having served on St. Joseph Hospital's Foundation board
of directors from 1989–1996, I felt that my association with the
hospital was over. A call from the dean of the College of
Business Administration at Augusta State University changed
all of that. Jack Widener, dean of the school and my boss at the

university, called me and asked me to serve on the hospital's board of directors. Jack was also serving as chairman of the hospital board.

Jack and I had been friends for years, dating back to the years when he and I both were in the corporate world with different companies. He was a senior executive with Georgia Power Company, and had enjoyed an outstanding record of public service in the community. Out of my deep respect for Jack, I welcomed the opportunity to serve with him outside of the university. St. Joseph Hospital's deep commitment to Christian principles also appealed to me. The hospital enjoys a reputation of being a Christ- centered institution that provides compassionate care to its patients. The board's composition was primarily made up of business leaders, lawyers, and physicians. There were no minorities serving on the board of directors. As a Christian, I found the work on the board very gratifying and rewarding.

Shortly after I joined the board of directors, I was asked to assume the chairmanship of the Finance Committee. My responsibility as chairman of this committee was consistent with my background in financial matters. Our charge was pretty clear-cut. The hospital, like most relatively small hospitals, was operating with a very thin margin. With major changes in the Medicare reimbursement formula, and stringent indemnification guidelines from insurers, St Joseph Hospital faced some cost-cutting challenges. Our meetings were stressful as we sought ways to earn a small profit. There were times when I wondered if we would be able to remain viable, before reminding myself of Saint Paul's admonition to continue to fight a good fight to the very end.

## *Healthcare Georgia Foundation Board of Directors (1999– )*

The Healthcare Georgia Foundation was created in 1999 as a result of an endowment in excess of one hundred million dollars from Blue Cross/Blue Shield of Georgia, subsequent to its conversion to a for-profit corporate structure. This endowment represented a commitment and preservation of public funds dedicated to improving the health of Georgians as a result of a class-action lawsuit contesting the company's conversion.

A nine-member board of directors was also provided for, and their primary role was to approve grants for the following nonprofit healthcare purposes: healthcare policy analysis, changes in the healthcare systems, and projects to improve healthcare for the uninsured. The board's composition was made up of three persons from the plaintiffs, three persons from the defendants, and three persons from the public sector. Following extended litigation, Blue Cross/Blue Shield appointed Dick Shirk, Charlie Underwood, and I to represent the defendants. The plaintiffs' members were Linda Lowe, Jerome Scott, and Mark Johnson. The public members were Enoch Prowe, James Curran, and Michael Kemp.

Putting behind the acrimony of litigation, the board was able to put aside its differences and work in a spirit of teamwork and cooperation. A major step toward our effectiveness as an organization occurred when the board recruited Dr. Gary Nelson as president and chief executive officer. Gary Nelson was recruited from California where he had enjoyed success as a leader in healthcare. Through his superb leadership, the Foundation assembled a highly skilled staff of professionals. The Foundation was able in a relatively short period of time to effect its mission to advance the health of all Georgians by awarding millions of dollars to this cause.

I take great delight in the Foundation's goal of addressing health disparities, strengthening nonprofit health organizations, and expanding access to healthcare.

Perhaps, through Healthcare Georgia, we can speed up the day when all the citizens of our state will have uninhibited access to healthcare.

# *Rotary Club of Augusta Board of Directors (2000– )*

I was surprised when Dr. James Puryear, from the Medical College of Georgia, called me in February 1985 to ask my permission for him to sponsor me for membership in Augusta's largest, most prestigious civic club. My surprise was due to the fact that most of the civic clubs in our area were largely segregated. He explained to me that he was committed to gaining my acceptance in the club, and that I would find one other African-American member in the Augusta Club, in the person of Dr. William Harris, President of Paine College.

I was warmly received as a member of the Rotary Club of Augusta on April 29, 1985. The origin of Rotary dates back to the day in 1900 when Paul Harris took a walk with one of his friends through the Rogers Park residential section of Chicago. During this walk, his friend stopped at several stores and shops and introduced Paul to his friends, the proprietors. This experience started Paul to wondering why he could not make social friends out of at least a few of his business friends. He later resolved to organize a club, which would band together a group of representative business and professional men in friendliness, comradeship, and understanding.

By 1905, after several years of reflecting on conditions of life and business, he had formulated a definite philosophy of business relations. After talking over his plans with three of his law clients, he decided, with them, to organize the club, which he had planned since 1900. On February 23, 1905, the first meeting of this club was held and his nucleus was formed for thousands of Rotary clubs, which were later organized throughout the world. Paul Harris named this new organization the Rotary club because originally the members met at various places of business. Rotary clubs have been organized and are now functioning in all the major countries and major geographical divisions of the world. The object of Rotary is to encourage and foster the ideal of service as a basis of worthy enterprise and, in particular, to encourage and foster the following principles: (1) The development of acquaintance as an opportunity for service. (2) High ethical standards in business and professions, the recognition of the worthiness of all useful occupations, and the dignifying by each Rotarian of his occupation as an opportunity to serve society. 3) The application of the ideal of service by every Rotarian to his personal, business, and community life. 4) The advancement of international understanding, goodwill, and peace through a world fellowship of business and professional people united in the ideal of service.

I embraced the principles of Rotary and sought to become an active service-oriented member. My election to the club's Board of Directors in 2000 also caught me by surprise. Shortly after my election to the board, several members of the club expressed the desire for me to become the club's first African-American president. Again, an unsolicited role of responsibility was placed on my shoulders. As of this writing, as the club's president-elect, I am ready to serve.

## *McDuffie Bank and Trust (1988– )*

As I prepared to travel to Atlanta for a Board of Regents meeting, I received a telephone call from Attorney Albert Dallas. Mr. Dallas asked me if I could meet with him at his home to discuss a very important confidential matter. At the meeting, Mr. Dallas informed me that a small group of people in the Thomson community was thinking about establishing a community bank and wanted me to become a part of the group. I told him that I would give it some thought and get back with him at a later date.

While driving to Atlanta I internalized the value of establishing another bank in the Thomson community and the added value of such a move. There were two banks in Thomson: Bank of Thomson and Trust Company Bank. These banks had been in business for over fifty years and enjoyed a loyal customer base. After considering whether I should participate in this highly speculative venture, I concluded that the positive value of my investment outweighed the negative value. As an organizing investor, it meant that a substantial amount of my personal assets would be required. I agreed to make an initial investment of $100,000.

The task of organizing a new bank was cumbersome. We had to petition the Georgia banking department for a charter, and demonstrate to the department that there was a need in the service area to establish a new bank. Additionally, the banking department's requirement of a minimum capitalization of $5,000,000 was no small feat. It also meant that we would have to assemble a group of committed organizers who would raise the required capital. The organizers were: Mary Ambrose, Richard Ambrose, Susan Dallas, Phillip Farr, Samuel Fowler, Jr., Alex Hobbs, George Hughes, David Joesbury, Charles Lewis, Mary Mohr, Patricia Lemley, Robert Wilson, Jr., Robert Wilson, Sr., Bennye Young, and I.

Our strategy was for each organizer to develop a prospect list of potential investors and solicit their investment in the bank. I wanted to assemble as many African-Americans as possible so that they too could enjoy the benefits of ownership of a local bank. To my dismay a lot of people, including close friends who I felt would participate, elected not to invest in this venture. On the other hand, a substantial number did invest. I was able to sell over $200,000 in shares of stock to African-American friends and associates.

We were successful in our efforts to raise the required capital and satisfy banking requirements for a new banking charter. Thus, we became the first new bank established in McDuffie County since 1902. Although there were subtle efforts from some of the major shareholders of the old established banks to keep our bank from opening, we successfully opened the bank earlier than the original projected period. Within a relatively short period of time, McDuffie Bank and Trust was operating in the black, with assets approaching $40 million.

Our success as a community bank attracted the attention of suitors and others who wanted to align themselves with our bank. Meanwhile, after reaching the $40 million plateau in Thomson-McDuffie County, our growth began to soften. We then began to plan strategies on our future. Ultimately, we formed a holding company, which created some flexibility opportunities for growth and expansion. In this regard, we formed an alliance with a group of prominent business leaders from Augusta, who infused millions of dollars of additional capital, and established offices in the Augusta market. Under the holding company umbrella of Georgia-Carolina Banchares, Incorporated, we accelerated our profits and asset size under the name of First Bank.

Through Georgia-Carolina Banchares, Incorporated, we assembled a board of directors who was highly successful and influential. In addition to the old directors from McDuffie Bank and Trust, the following directors provided governance for the company: Patrick Blanchard, Remer Brinson, Larry DeMeyers, Arthur Gay, Jr., J. Randal Hall, Hugh Hamilton, Jr., William Hatcher, George Inman, John Lee, A. Montague Miller, and Julian Osbon. Within a short span of time, First Bank had achieved the distinction of being the fastest-growing community bank in Georgia, and one of the best-performing banks in the country, as our assets exceeded $300 million.

## *Boys and Girls Club (2001– )*

Having taken on so many assignments from various organizations, I told my wife that I would not accept any more invitations to serve on boards. My calendar was too heavy. I told her that I was going to resist the nagging guilt of saying "no" when asked to serve. I thought my resolve to say "no" was solid, until I received a call to meet with a group of community leaders in Thomson to discuss the plight of the boys and girls in our community.

The convener discussed the number of teen pregnancies, school delinquencies, and growing crime among the youth in our community. He offered those of us in attendance an opportunity to do something about the problem by forming a Boys and Girls Club. Without a second thought, I volunteered to serve as a member of the organizing board of directors.

Our initial efforts to get the organization off the ground seemed futile. We did not have any facilities, money, or other needed resources. However, through the generosity of several community leaders we were able to move into borrowed quarters, acquire some used furniture, and get moving. Before long, we had more kids signing up for participation than we could accommodate. Much of the credit for our initial success can be attributed to a small cadre of unselfish leaders, such as our city and county governing elected officials, who provided funds and grants to construct an attractive facility in the heart of the minority community with a value in excess of a half million dollars. Our president, Anne Knox, provided visionary leadership during this period of transition.

Although the Boys and Girls Clubs touch only a fraction of the lives of our youth, the sacrifice of time and energy is a sound investment in our future. In this regard, the mission statement sums up the true value of our effort: "To inspire and enable all young people, especially those in disadvantaged circumstances, to realize their full potential as productive, responsible, and caring citizens."

*Chapter Ten*

# INSIDE THE BOARD OF REGENTS' GOVERNANCE

FOLLOWING THE SWEARING-IN ceremony and the photo session, we were escorted to the Regents' Building at 244 Washington Street. Having been a regent for only fifteen minutes, it was time to go to work. I entered the elevator to go up to the fifth floor where the regents held their meetings, where to my surprise, the lady on the elevator asked, "Sir, aren't you Regent Greene?" My reply was, "No, I'm Joseph Greene."

The first few minutes dealt primarily with whether or not our thirty-three colleges and universities should remain on the quarter system or change to the semester system. My position: in order to have some form of continuity, all of the units should be on the same system ... keeping the quarter system. Another major concern was whether we would lose $125 million in federal funds due to our failure to fully desegregate our system. The governor and Attorney General Mike Bowers had a strong plea for full compliance. Finally, the Office of Civil Rights (OCR) approved our desegregation plan.

Chancellor Vernon Crawford announced his retirement and the field quickly was crowded with candidates, including Dean Propst, Executive Vice Chancellor, and Dr. Fred Davison, President of the University of Georgia. Strong lobbying on behalf of Fred Davison occurred and I personally resented the strong-armed, arrogant approach that some of his supporters used. I decided that he was Not My Choice. His apparent indifference during the desegregation debate kept haunting me, and I did not see a commitment in him to correct the past inequities. The regents cast their votes for chancellor: Dean Propst received twelve votes, and Fred Davison received three votes.

Dr. Davison did not like our decision. Shortly after our decision, Dr. Davison announced that President Reagan was considering him for U.S. Secretary of Education, and that he would likely accept the appointment. He later invited the three regents who voted for him to accompany the university's football team delegation to the Tangerine Bowl, as the Bulldog's guests, as the University of Georgia's Bulldogs appeared in the Tangerine Bowl in Florida. This decision infuriated several regents as an act of reprisal and alienated some of them from Dr. Davison.

Throughout the early months of my tenure, I felt inadequate much of the time. I did not feel on top of the issues, I did not feel comfortable in handling the massive amount of materials, budget statistics, etc. My peers seemed well prepared; they were successful men and women and displayed confidence in their deliberations as regents. I was later to come to the realization that that my frame of reference had trapped me. That is, having served on the McDuffie County Board of Education for thirteen years, I felt a high degree of expertise. I commanded statewide respect through my directorship on the Georgia School Boards Association. I was vice chairman of the Board of Education—but a rookie on the Board of Regents ... and rookies are not to speak and they are not to know ... they are to watch and listen and learn!

PAINFUL, PAINFUL!!!

There existed a loose coalition of Governor Harris's appointees and the holdover regents from the previous administration. My views, philosophically speaking, were more in line with the Harris appointees: Regents John Henry Anderson, Arthur Gignilliat, Jackie Ward, and Elridge McMillian and I were on the same wavelength on equal-opportunity issues.

## *Division among the Regents*

When Dr. John Skandalakis, Chairman of the Board of Regents, expressed his desire to offer for chairmanship for another year, Governor Harris's appointees rejected the idea. In my opinion, Regent Skandalakis was too close to Dr. Fred Davison at the University of Georgia, and had not demonstrated his support for the our new chancellor, Dr. Dean Propst. The other regents offered Regent Skandalakis and Regent McMillan as chairman and vice chairman. Governor Harris appointees offered Regents Arthur Gignilliat and John Anderson as chairman and vice chairman. My support of the Harris teams' officers was solid ... notwithstanding that an African-American was being offered for vice chairman, in Regent McMillian.

Prior to our meeting, I spoke with Regent Elridge McMillan, an African-American, and explained to him why I would not support his candidacy. I nominated Regent John Henry Anderson for vice chairman, but when the votes were counted, Regent Elridge McMillian had won. Although my nominee had lost, I felt good on the inside knowing Regent Eldridge McMillian would become the first African-American vice chairman of the Board of Regents.

## *Controversy at the University of Georgia*

Dr. Jan Kemp, an English Professor at the University of Georgia, filed a lawsuit against Dr. Virginia Trotter and Dr. Leroy Erwin, charging that she had been fired because she protested preferential treatment for athletes. The lawsuit resulted in a guilty verdict, and a judgment of $2.5 million in damages against the University of Georgia. Everything started to unravel at the University of Georgia. The Board of Regents ordered an internal audit at the university to ascertain the validity of the allegations. Meanwhile, Dr. Fred Davison, president of the university denied any knowledge or involvement. The Board of Regents decided to hold off on Dr. Davison's reappointment as president until we had an opportunity to study the audit. The media relished the controversy. The *Wall*

*Street Journal, Washington Post, Atlanta Constitution*, NBC, CBS, ABC, AP, UPI … No time was sacred. I had calls from the media for comments up until midnight and on weekends. My stated position: "As regents we must, at all cost, uphold academic integrity. Those who are guilty must be relieved of their responsibility." Dr. Fred Davison did not like our delaying his appointment until the audit was completed. He announced his resignation from the University of Georgia. A small number of the regents attempted to get the Board of Regents to relent and appeal to Dr. Davison to withdraw his resignation. However, a majority of the regents were unwilling to ask Dr. Davison to remain. There was a statewide lobbying effort by some of Dr. Davison's supporters to pressure the regents to reject his letter of resignation. I received dozens of letters daily about the controversy. My mail was very heavily in favor of retaining Dr. Davison as president. Political figures visited my office and/or called me on behalf of Dr. Davison. Given all that had transpired at the University of Georgia, I remained convinced that Dr. Davison, as president, could not walk away from this controversy without accepting responsibility. My resolve stiffened to uphold academic integrity.

## *Augusta College Housing*

Augusta College's mission was to serve as a commuter college when it was founded. However, times had changed and students who did not have transportation could attend college if the college had on-campus housing. Dr. George Christenberry, President of Augusta College, convinced me to support his efforts to establish student housing on campus.

My fellow regents, under intense lobbying from the Summerville neighborhood organization, rejected campus housing. I felt devastated and shattered. I had lost fourteen to one. However in losing, I remained convinced that the Summerville neighborhood organization did not want minorities living in that area, and the issue of the college's mission gave them a convenient cover to mount their opposition. My daughter, Cathy, sensed my frustration and said to me, "Dad, I'm proud of what you did today." She had watched the news on television and she knew how badly I wanted housing for those students at Augusta College.

Having wrestled with these issues and others, I no longer felt intimidated by the office or the job. My comfort level had risen and I commanded attention when I spoke. Still, there was so much more about this job that I did not know. I occasionally felt that perhaps there was more thought into a regent's seven-year term than meets the eye.

## History is Made

In June of 1986, the Board of Regents made history in electing its first African-American as chairman. I felt good about the election of Regent Elridge McMillian to the chairmanship of the Board of Regents. Our coalition supported his candidacy along with Regent Jackie Ward as vice chairperson. Regent McMillian, who was appointed by Governor George Busbee, was extremely knowledgeable about higher education and would employ his knowledge in leading the university system of Georgia.

## The Medical College of Georgia

What a humbling position ... A feeling of frustration followed my passionate appeal for the Buildings and Grounds committee to endorse Dr. Jesse Steinfeld, president of the Medical College of Georgia, Master Plan for the Medical College of Georgia expansion. The committee decided to study the plan for later consideration. The delaying tactic did not bother me as much as my inability to get the committee to vote on an issue that I considered vital to the Medical College of Georgia. Meanwhile, the full Board of Regents considered the Augusta College foundation's land swap proposal in order to construct off-campus housing. Again, several regents balked and wanted to reject the request on "the basis of changing the mission." No! I was not going to give in an inch. I chided them for their "inconsistency and sending mixed signals."

The request passed ... some solace!

In the spring of 1987, Dr. Jesse Steinfeld, President of the Medical College of Georgia, announced his resignation due to health reasons. I was saddened. Dr. Steinfeld was such a strong president, straightforward and full of integrity. While his health—he was diagnosed with a degenerative disease—was failing, I was sure his critics played a large part in his leaving. The basis of his tragic flaw was that he attempted to lead the institution in the direction of its mission of education and service. His efforts met with a great deal of opposition. For instance, the Physician Practice Group had fared well under previous administrations in charting their own course, which led to economic prosperity for the Practice Group. Dr. Steinfeld did not yield to the "Good Ole Boy" network. The lobbying started as people sought to influence me on appointing an interim president for the Medical College of Georgia.

The Board of Regents' policy on presidential searches requires the local institution to form a campus search committee to work concurrently with a regents' search committee. Earlier, I chaired the search committee for the new president of Augusta College. Dr. Stephen Hobbs, Professor at Augusta College, led the college's search committee through a marvelous job of selecting and recommending Dr. Richard Wallace to the Regents' committee, which was chaired by me. Dr. Wallace was the finalist out of a pool of 164 candidates. Meanwhile, I was also serving on the University of Georgia Search Committee under Regent Sidney Smith. We finally selected Dr. Charles Knapp from Tulane as the new president of the University of Georgia.

## Regent's Office

At our May 13, 1987 meeting, I had a deep feeling that I would emerge as a candidate for vice chairman of the board. I even did a head count and felt that I had the votes, if nominated. However, I could never bring myself to the point of solicitation.

Regents Jackie Ward, John Henry Anderson, Elridge McMillian, Chancellor Propst, and I had a meeting with Governor Harris in his office on the Medical College of

Georgia expansion project. Following our meeting with Governor Harris, Regents Ward and Anderson asked me if I would accept the vice chairmanship. I told them that if elected, I would serve. The effort was underway to support me as vice chairman. I made no contacts, calls, or requests, but knew that Jackie Ward and John Henry Anderson were lining up support.

At the June 9–10, 1987 meeting, it was obvious that Jackie Ward and John Henry Anderson had successfully lobbied the regents to support me as vice chairman. Jackie Ward was elected chairperson. John Henry Anderson nominated me, and two other regents seconded the nomination simultaneously ... I was in as vice chairman of the board. What a humbling and touching moment. Just five days earlier, I had delivered the commencement speech at Emanuel County Junior College in Swainsboro, Georgia, where I'd attended segregated schools, and was now speaking to an integrated audience and becoming vice chairman of the University System Board of Regents.

The headlines in Augusta Chronicle told the story, "Greene in Line to Become Second Black Chairman of Georgia Regents Board":

> Joseph D. Greene's election Wednesday as the Vice Chairman of the Georgia Board of Regents places the Thomson resident in line to become the second black to ever head the governing body for the state's university system ... Greene is not new to historical precedence, being the first black elected official in McDuffie county, as a member of the school board.

In reflecting over the years of debates, frustrations, and disenchantment with some of my fellow regents, I found that I had to learn to separate issues from people and personalities and not to become a hostage of my own feelings and emotions.

On February 10, 1988, Governor Joe Frank Harris appointed two new regents, Dean Day Smith and Barry Phillips. They replaced Marie Dodd and John Skandalakis. Skandalakis had written me a warm letter in response to my sending him a poem ("A Living Dream"), during his illness.

## Fort Valley State College's Turmoil

Dr. Luther Burse, President of Fort Valley State College had been under fire. It seemed that he had been unable to mobilize a supporting constituency in the white community, and to silence the group of internal dissidents. Further, Regent John Henry Anderson had been a conduit in which factions had voiced opposition. I feared that Regent Anderson had become too close to the turmoil and had become biased. At any rate, the chancellor had given President Burse a negative evaluation, which meant his departure was imminent.

I did not feel that President Burse had received an objective assessment of his leadership at the institution. Some of his critics were powerful leaders in the Fort Valley area, and had galvanized an extensive lobbying effort to remove him from office. Although I vehemently opposed his removal, again, I was in the minority and lost.

## Disproportionate Appointments

I expressed my disappointment in our meeting over the fact that out of fifty-two faculty appointments, there was a glaring absence of females and minorities. For example, up for appointment considerations were thirty-four white men, fourteen women, two African-Americans, and two Asian-Americans.

Following my comments to the Board, I passed a note to Regent Carolyn Yancey, an African-American, relative to my comments on the Board to express my disappointment over the small number of minorities hired: "Carolyn, I am extremely concerned about the small number of minority appointments. This issue will require our close continued scrutiny." Carolyn: "You are right. It's well to continue mentioning it."

Early in 1988, there was a backlog of highly charged issues for the Regents to address. For instance, Dr. Wendell Rayburn, President of Savannah State College, resigned his presidency. While there were lobbyists from Savannah urging me to get involved in the Savannah State search, I was chairman of the Medical College of Georgia Presidential Search Committee and did not want to interfere in the Savannah search. The Medical College of Georgia search was quite difficult, due to the large number of internal candidates, including my friend, Dr. Fran Tedesco.

Another critical issue of concern facing the regents was desegregation. United States Secretary of Education William Bennett had charged Georgia with noncompliance in desegregating our colleges and universities. Our efforts to attract white students at Albany State College, Fort Valley State College, and Savannah State College had not been highly successful. I often thought to myself how tough the job of being a regent had become. There was no shortage of critical issues.

## *Merger Proposal*

No controversial issues were on the March 8–9, 1988 agenda, just the routine issues. However, what emerged was anything but routine. During a briefing by the chancellor to the Executive Committee (Regents Jackie Ward, Elridge McMillan, Arthur Gignilliat, John Henry Anderson, and I) on presidential searches, the chancellor commented that perhaps we should be considering some mergers. He advanced the idea of merging Albany Junior College, a traditionally white college, into Albany State College, a historically black college, and Armstrong State College, a historically white college, with Savannah State College, a historically black college. The chancellor suggested this merger idea to the full Board during our meeting. The Board authorized a study with an interim report due the next month. The Savannah State College Alumni set off a charge of opposition. Their fear was, as in the past, blacks would come up short on any merger. They argued that history supported this precedent. Meanwhile, I had accepted an invitation to briefly speak at the regional Savannah State College Alumni meeting the following Saturday in Augusta. They were polite to me, but very firm and emotional in their opposition to any merger attempt. I urged them to maintain an open mind and express their views as objectively as possible. I thought to myself, this is going to be a tough ride!

At our April 12–13, 1988 meeting, no other issue, with the exceptions of Jan Kemp and Fred Davison, had created as much discussion as had the proposed merger of Savannah State College with Armstrong State College, and Albany State College with Albany Junior College. In this regard, our April meeting held at Fort Valley State College was a test of nerves and emotions. The chancellor, Dean Propst, had held public meetings in Savannah and Albany and had given local citizens space on the April agenda to express their views of opposition. Their views were highly emotional. Our meeting closed with the promise that we would make a final decision at the May meeting. The letters started rolling in … with the comments "do not merge" these colleges.

My own view led me to conclude that although it was hard to justify, economically, two separate institutions in these cities, there were other considerations. Clearly, the six thousand-plus students who attended the historically black colleges in Georgia were better off at smaller, historically black colleges. These colleges were highly sensitive to their plight, and better prepared to respond. Many were admitted with academic deficiencies, low SAT scores, etc. They needed special attention, which they would not get at a predominantly white school. Dr. Jacqueline Fleming's book *Blacks and Higher Education* articulated the pressures of college in general, and especially for African-Americans who needed to participate and to identify a mentor on campus. On the balance, putting economics aside, I felt that we were better off keeping these colleges separate. The regents' vote not to merge brought a sigh of relief from a packed house.

In the meantime, we were bringing the presidential search to a conclusion at the Medical College of Georgia. From a national pool of 130 candidates, we settled on four individuals as finalists. Although I felt that any of the the four finalists would make outstanding presidents, I favored Dr. Francis Tedesco, Acting Dean of the School of Medicine at the Medical College of Georgia. It was a close vote within the committee between Dr. Tedesco and Dr. Charles Putnam of Duke University School of Medicine.

After agreeing to appoint Dr. Tedesco as president of the Medical College of Georgia, we did the usual protocol. We held a press conference and answered questions as to why we selected Dr. Tedesco. I felt certain that we had made a wise decision and that the Medical College was in good hands. As we wrapped up this presidential search, some of my fellow regents reminded me that I would be elected chairman of the board of Regents at our June meeting.

*Chapter Eleven*

# ELECTED CHAIRMAN

AT OUR BOARD MEETING of June 7–8, 1988, with a unanimous vote, led by Regent John Henry Anderson's motion, seconded by Regent Elridge McMillian, I became chairman of the Board of Regents. Regent Edgar Rhodes from Bremen was elected vice chairman. A large delegation of family and friends from Thomson traveled to Atlanta to witness the occasion. Those who were in attendance: Barney and David (Cathy was at UGA taking her finals), Rev. F. D. Favors, Clara West, Rosezenia Culpepper, Lucille Paschal, Dorothy Logan, Grace Tyson, Margaret Harris, Alma Perry, and Lena Thomas. As David, my son, and I walked to the bathroom he asked, "Dad, when you finish as chairman of the Board of Regents, what are you going to do?" I replied, "Son, I don't know! He said, "Why don't you run for governor?" It was not impossible ... and for my nine-year-old son to think in those terms meant a lot to me. It meant that he saw no barriers due to his race. My efforts, as chairman, would be one of seeking full accessibility and opportunity for everyone, especially minorities who had been excluded. The full impact of my election had not dawned on me yet; I felt a little numb. My acceptance remarks follows:

YOU HAVE GIVEN ME TODAY, AN OPPORTUNITY TO DO WHAT ONLY A FEW GEORGIANS WILL EVER DO ... TO SERVE AS CHAIRMAN OF THE BOARD OF REGENTS OF THE UNIVERSITY SYSTEM OF GEORGIA. I WANT TO THANK YOU FOR YOUR VOTE OF CONFIDENCE IN ME AND MY LEADERSHIP ABILITY. PLEASE JOIN ME IN EXTENDING A STANDING OVATION OF APPRECIA-

TION TO REGENT JACKIE WARD FOR THE EXCELLENT LEADER-
SHIP SHE HAS OFFERED DURING HER TENURE AS CHAIRPERSON.
SHE HAS OFFERED VISIONARY AND DECISIVE LEADERSHIP ...
AND WE ARE INDEBTED TO HER.

THERE ARE SO MANY PEOPLE THAT I WOULD LIKE TO
THANK FOR THEIR CONTINUING SUPPORT IN MY MANY
ENDEAVORS:

MY WIFE AND CHILDREN
FAMILY MEMBERS
CHURCH FAMILY
MY COMPANY—THE PILGRIM
H & L INS. CO

THEIR SUPPORT HAS SUSTAINED ME THROUGH SOME DIF-
FICULT TIMES.

OUR COUNTRY IS FAR FROM PERFECT AND SO IS OUR SYS-
TEM ... BUT I SUBMIT TO YOU THAT PROGRESS IS BEING MADE
DAILY ... ON MANY FRONTS. AS I APPROACHED THIS DAY, I
COULD NOT HELP BUT REFLECT ON THE PAST ... AND MY OWN
EXPERIENCES IN EDUCATION.

GRADUATING FROM A SEGREGATED HIGH SCHOOL THIRTY
YEARS AGO, THERE WERE ONLY THREE PUBLIC COLLEGES IN
GEORGIA OPEN TO ME, BECAUSE OF MY COLOR. AND THE
THREE WERE CLOSED IN A SENSE BECAUSE I DID NOT HAVE THE
MONEY TO ATTEND THEM.

HOWEVER, FOLLOWING YEARS OF EMPLOYMENT, AND
SERVICE IN THE U.S. ARMY DURING THE VIETNAM WAR, I WAS
ABLE TO JOIN THE FIRST GROUP OF BLACK STUDENTS WHO
GAINED ADMISSION TO AUGUSTA COLLEGE.

THERE WERE GOOD EXPERIENCES, AND SOME THAT ARE
BEST LEFT UNSHARED WITH YOU. HOWEVER, I SAW A COMMIT-
MENT ON THE PART OF SOME ON THAT CAMPUS TO MAKE EDU-
CATION ACCESSIBLE TO ALL STUDENTS ... WITHOUT REGARD
TO THEIR DIFFERENCES. I SAW GOOD DECENT AMERICAN PRO-
FESSORS, WHO EXTENDED THEMSELVES TO HELP STUDENTS
WHO WERE DISADVANTAGED.

I HAVE WITNESSED IN A GENERATION, PROGRESS THAT MY
FATHER, WHO DIED NEARLY TWENTY-FIVE YEARS AGO, DARED
NOT TO DREAM OF ...

MY FELLOW REGENTS, THAT'S ENOUGH ABOUT THE PAST.

TODAY, THERE ARE MILLIONS OF GEORGIANS WHOSE
LIVES WILL BE AFFECTED BY OUR COLLECTIVE LEADERSHIP.
THIS IS AN ENORMOUS RESPONSIBILITY ... THAT WE SHARE
TOGETHER.

IN THE WORDS OF WINSTON CHURCHILL, "TODAY WE
SHAPE OUR INSTITUTIONS BY WHAT WE DO AND TOMORROW,
WE ARE SHAPED BY THEM."

I BELIEVE IN ALL OF YOU ...

I BELIEVE IN OUR GREAT SYSTEM.

I BELIEVE IN OUR GREAT STATE

AND

I BELIEVE TOGETHER, WE CAN SHAPE

OUR INSTITUTIONS AS WELL.

THANK YOU ALL.

Letters cards, telephone calls, and expressions of best wishes came from everywhere. People stopped me on the streets to
extend their congratulations on my becoming chairman of the
board. The news media, from Jet Magazine to Swainsboro's
*Forest Blade* newspaper carried the story. My employer, The
Pilgrim Health and Life Insurance Company, hosted a reception on July 22, 1988 at the Holiday Inn, poolside, in
Augusta in my honor. A large crowd attended, including
soul singer James Brown. Further, Georgia State University
and The First National Bank of Atlanta hosted a reception for
me on August 9, 1988, in Atlanta. Attorney Buddy Dallas,
County Attorney for McDuffie County informed me that the
county would have a special day of recognition in my honor
on August 3, 1988.

My first official act, as chairman, was to meet with Henry
Neal, Executive Secretary of the Board of Regents for the purpose of appointing committees.

## *Tenure as Chairman*

I chaired my first meeting as chairman of the Board of
Regents on August 9, 1988. With my saying "The meeting will
please come to order," my first meeting as chairman of the
board was underway (see Appendix). The meeting agenda was

pretty routine; I presented a plaque to Regent Jackie Ward in recognition of her having served as chairperson. The issue of Dr. Luther Burse, President of Fort Valley State College, and pending resignation was discussed in Executive Session. His resignation was scheduled to take effect September 2, 1988. I pressed to delay the date until June 30, 1989. With the recent court decree on desegregation, the vacancy at Savannah State College, in my opinion, made for bad timing. However, Regent John Henry Anderson was adamantly opposed to delaying the date. A consensus of the Board agreed with Regent Anderson. However, the matter remained alive.

The Fort Valley State College controversy remained the focal issue. The National Alumni Association, headed by Tommy Dortch, aide to Senator Sam Nunn, had requested to be placed on the meeting agenda. A delegation, led by Mr. Dortch, appeared before the Executive Committee. A large delegation of supporters of Dr. Burse from Fort Valley requested the reinstatement of Luther Burse as president. We gave them thirty minutes on the agenda to express their views. Following an emotional presentation by the delegation, I thanked them for their views and stated that a change in administration should not be construed as a lack of support for the college, and that "I fully appreciate the college's heritage and will work to continue its viability." They were not happy!

Our budget was on the agenda for submission to the General Assembly; a 34 percent increase in funding was proposed. Although we held out little hope of getting the funds requested, I argued that we should convey our true needs to the General Assembly. The *Augusta Chronicle* newspaper in its September 9, 1988 issue carried a favorable editorial in support of my position.

I felt comfortable with my new role and would try to affect the concept of strategic planning, greater accessibility to minorities in enrollment and employment, and a prepaid tuition plan.

At our November 8–9, 1988 meeting, the Fort Valley State College issue was no longer front-page news. There were only light discussions about the changes at the college. A new issue, pertaining to whether we would grant university status to

Georgia Southern College and Valdosta State College, was now the central issue.

As I settled into my tenure as chairman, I was receiving invitations to speak throughout the state of Georgia. Civic clubs such as Rotary, Kiwanis, Optimists, churches, and colleges extended me speaking invitations. Among the highlight of the many speeches that I made was the commencement address at Georgia State University before an audience of five to six thousand, including 1,300 graduates. I spoke on "Facing Your Destiny." My comments were designed to challenge the graduates to prepare themselves for new challenges in the world. If it were not for the regents' communications director, Kay Miller, who wrote most of my speeches, I could not have fulfilled the many invitations.

Our December 13–14, 1988 meeting was very special in that my wife, Barney, and our daughter, Cathy, attended the meeting. Cathy, home for Christmas break from the University of Georgia, wanted to attend to observe me presiding as chairman. Barney went along in order to attend a party being given by Regent Dean Day Smith. Later, Cathy wrote me a note in which she said she was extremely proud to see her father presiding … and commented on how fortunate she felt to have parents like us. Deep inside I thanked God for Cathy and the joy that she had brought into our lives.

The regional university issue was still being debated. We were scheduled to make some definite decisions in our January meeting. Meanwhile, the Medical College of Georgia's $37 million project was still in a delicate state in terms of funding. While enabling legislation was enacted, no state funds were involved. Rather, a General Obligation Bond was the route we were pursuing. I met with Governor Harris personally on behalf of this project and said, "Governor, you've got to help me on this project; otherwise I'll get a black eye in Augusta."

The governor smiled and responded, "No I'll get one. We're going to work with you—we are looking at how we're going to do it." While this issue at the Medical College claimed my attention, Augusta College held groundbreaking ceremonies for its new gymnasium and student-housing complex on Wrightsboro Road. I represented the Board of Regents with remarks and participated in the groundbreaking ceremony. I was really enjoying my tenure—being in the middle of, and orchestrating, higher education for our state was really exciting. Speaking engagements, commencements, and academic awards, were still flowing in to me from throughout Georgia.

I had gotten dozens of letters from South Georgia in support of our creating Regional Universities in the Valdosta and Statesboro areas. The chancellor prepared a draft, in which he pointed out that the time had evolved, along with economic growth in South Georgia, to create these universities. When I gaveled the meeting to order, there were fourteen state senators and House representatives in attendance. They were there to lobby the regents to support establishing Regional Universities. The chancellor's recommendation for the designation passed unanimously. The media was there too, in large numbers! I appointed a Presidential Search Committee for Fort Valley State College. Regents Bill Turner, Chairman; Carolyn Yancey; and John Henry Anderson were asked to serve on the search committee. The other main thrust at this point was centered on our budget from the General Assembly. In this regard, the chancellor asked me to accompany him to plead our case before the Senate-House Appropriations Committee on Tuesday, January 17, 1989, at 1:40 p.m. The chancellor made an effective presentation to the legislative committee, and we responded to their questions.

Meanwhile, Regent Elridge McMillian had been chairing a special committee on increasing minority participation in the university system. The committee had recommended some bold approaches and they were unanimously approved by the full board. We spent a great deal of time assessing the chancellor's evaluation of all of the college presidents before renewing employment contracts. Dr. Pat Crecine, President of Georgia Tech, did not receive a favorable evaluation. He had caused the chancellor some problems in the media by criticizing the funding formula for Georgia Tech.

Following our Tuesday board meeting, I went to the governor's office for a private meeting with him. I thanked Governor Harris for his support of the Medical College of Georgia expansion project ($37 million) and his overall support of the university system. He thanked my fellow regents and me for our contributions as well. Following this meeting, I visited with several legislators with courtesy calls. In addition to my responsibilities as chairman of the Board of Regents, my normal speaking agenda was getting heavier. My speech at the University of Georgia's Minority Visitation Day program to five or six hundred students and faculty, on a Saturday, was typical of even weekend commitments. This appearance was followed by my participation on the alumni panel the next Saturday at the University of Georgia on the issue of "Demographics & Access."

On March 1, 1989, returning from Fort Valley State College where I had made a special presentation, the chancellor was on the phone when I arrived home. The chancellor wanted me to call a special called meeting of the Board to refuse the request of the Atlanta Constitution newspaper's bid to gain access to all of the files on the Georgia State University Presidential Search, under the Open Records Act. We held that we had an obligation to protect the confidentiality of candidates. Following our meeting, we went to the state capital to meet with Lt. Governor Zell Miller, who had blocked a House amendment to exempt the Board of Regents from the Open Records Act. He objected to the regents' approach and restated his opposition in letting the Senate consider the amendment. Additionally, Attorney General Mike Bowers, who normally would represent the Regents in litigation, had indicated that he would not defend our position. Having the state attorney general rebuff our efforts, we made a request to Governor Harris to appoint outside counsel to represent the Board of Regents, should the newspaper file a suit against us. The governor appointed counsel to represent us. We ultimately lost in the appeal to Georgia's Supreme Court 4 to 3. We asked the Supreme Court to reconsider its narrow decision.

We held our April meeting at West Georgia College in Carrollton. The major issue of discussion was the Georgia State Presidential Search. The media was anxious to know who was going to be appointed. We met in Executive Session and appointed Dr. John Palms as our new president. A press conference was held later in Atlanta. Following the press conference, we took Dr. Palms to Georgia State University to introduce him to faculty, staff, and students. The chancellor and I made introductory remarks about Dr. Palm.

During our May 9–10, 1989 meeting, Regent Bill Divine's replacement was sworn in at 11:00 a.m. in the governor's office. As chairman of the board, I welcomed Regent John Clark from Moultrie, Georgia as our newest regent. We also officially welcomed Dr. John Palms, Georgia State University's new president, to our university system. During our meeting, we received word that the Georgia Supreme Court had refused to reconsider our open-record request relative to Presidential Searches. We named a new president at Middle Georgia College. Meanwhile, my tenure as chairman was winding down. I had mixed emotions at this point.

As I approached June 13–14, 1989, my final days as chairman of the board, I experienced mixed emotions. I was mentally tired from the many issues that I had to deal with as chairman—the letters, phone calls, speeches, appearances, and leadership requirements—yet I knew deep down inside that I would miss the internal charge, the challenges and the exhilaration of leading the university system. For instance, my commencement speech on Saturday, June 10, 1989, before an audience of 7,500 at Georgia Southern College (one thousand-plus graduates), was a most gratifying experience.

Our agenda was routine, except for the discovery of a $3 million shortage in auxiliary funds at Valdosta State College. The funds were lost through an investment brokerage firm operating out of Arkansas. Regent Edgar Rhodes was elected chairman and John Henry Anderson was elected vice chairman. I thanked my fellow regents and staff for their cooperation during my tenure. They gave me a standing ovation for my leadership. Meanwhile, the chancellor reminded me that I was still chairman through June 30, 1989.

In reflecting on the major things accomplished during my tenure, the following come to mind:

1. Emphasis on strategic planning, with a clear mission of what our priorities were (education, research, and serv-

ice), and how resources could be channeled in this direction.

2. Increased minority participation in higher education in all areas.
3. The Medical College of Georgia expansion project of $37 million.
4. The cessation of monitoring by the Office of Civil Rights due to our compliance.
5. A modest tuition increase of 4 percent.
6. An improved and objective evaluation system for personnel.
7. The Augusta College housing opening and Athletic Complex development.

Disappointments:

1. Faculty salaries.
2. Opening presidential searches to the public.

*Chapter Twelve*

# END OF TENURE

ON JULY 11, 1989, as I walked from the Capitol parking lot to the regents meeting, I thought of how it felt to have been to the top, with all the responsibilities, the perks, the pressure ... and then the feeling of letdown when it was all over. My private parking space in the Regents building had been relinquished to the new chairman, Regent Edgar Rhodes, serving notice that my tenure as chairman had come to an end. I felt a sense of relief, though, knowing that my tenure as chairman was over. And more importantly, I was pleased with the results. I felt that I had presided with dignity. My fellow regents presented me with a plaque and made complimentary remarks to me. I found my seat among my fellow Regents for deliberations.

The primary discussion issue centered on the Regional University issue at Georgia Southern College. With a pending vote on Georgia Southern College becoming a Regional University, in which Savannah State College and Armstrong State College would be affiliated via their graduate programs, interest had intensified. Regent Elridge McMillian had written a dissenting position statement. Savannah State College's national alumni association had a large delegation in attendance to oppose the elevation of Georgia Southern. They feared that Savannah State's historical mission would be jeopardized. While I experienced mixed emotions, the momentum was such that Georgia Southern College's elevation was sealed—and those benefits from the affiliation could be beneficial to Savannah State College. Following extended debate, Regent McMillian offered a substitute motion to elevate

Georgia Southern College but to leave the Savannah Colleges off the merger list. I seconded the motion. The motion failed. Regent Arthur Gignilliat prevailed when Regents McMillian and Yancey voted against the proposal and I abstained. My abstaining was to convey support for Georgia Southern College's elevation to university status, while opposing the affiliation of Savannah State College. Meanwhile, we were able to place The Medical College of Georgia's Children Hospital on the Capital Priority list. The chancellor feared that we were asking for too much. I argued that all of our needs should be requested and prioritized. I left Atlanta with a feeling of accomplishment ... feeling good on the inside because I had held my principles intact.

Our December 12–13, 1989 agenda was pretty routine with the exception of an appearance by the Rev. Joseph Lowery, President of the Southern Christian Leadership Conference, on behalf of Savannah State College, to protest the elevation of Georgia Southern to university status. A rather large delegation from Savannah State accompanied Rev. Lowery. While the board listened with courtesy, my feeling was that the issue was closed and not to be visited again. On the funding side, from all indications, our budget was going to be tight the next year and we would have to lobby with the legislature to fund our requests. The Medical College would break ground for the new $36 million ambulatory care unit on the next Tuesday, in which I represented the Board of Regents with remarks.

On January 9–10, 1990, two of my fellow regents, John Henry Anderson and Arthur Gignilliat, were sworn in for a second seven-year term. By now, I was more keenly aware of the importance of our roles as Regents and guardians of higher education and protectors of Georgia's economic quality of life. Chancellor Propst delivered his state of the University System message. We faced some critical choices as we approached the year 2000.

As we prepared to reappoint presidents for the various institutions, Dr. Jerry Williamson's reappointment as president of Gordon College was doubtful. Dr. Williamson had been charged with acts of racism and sexism. We had received dozens of letters from disgruntled faculty members as well as supporters about Dr. Williamson's leadership. In response to the complaints, the chancellor had conducted an investigation and discovered that many of the allegations were true. However, Dr. Propst wanted to reappoint Dr. Williamson, with a provision that major reforms must be initiated at the college. However, Regents Jackie Ward, John Henry Anderson, and I felt that he should be terminated. The three of us therefore voted against his reelection. My statement to the media: "While I applaud the chancellor's efforts to resolve the problem at Gordon College, I feel that it is in the College's best interest and the University System's best interest to make a change in administration." My objection did not prevail, Dr. Williamson was reappointed with the Regents voting 8:3:1:0. The other presidents were routinely reappointed.

We held our spring meeting on April 10–11, 1990, at the Medical College of Georgia. The campus atmosphere was festive and upbeat. Dr. Fran Tedesco, President, had planned a number of special events for the regents, including dinner in honor of the regents at the Pinnacle Club in Augusta. My wife, Barney, took time off from school in order to participate with the regents' spouses during the various social events. The major topic for discussion was a 4 percent increase in tuition for the university system's students. We also approved a faculty salary increase of 4 percent. The regents all expressed dismay and frustration over the fact that we were not in a position to grant a larger salary increase. I had pressed for a 9 percent increase earlier. We also decided to extend the term of office for our chairman and vice-chairman of the Board of Regents to a minimum of two years. Regent Jackie Ward and I were in our final year as regents, and she and I discussed our situation in terms of our likely departure from the board. With a new governor taking office next January, it was likely that we would not be reappointed. It was a precarious situation for me in that several of the gubernatorial candidates had approached me to support their candidacy. As I assessed the situation, I was leaning toward supporting former congressman Andrew Young. I admired Mr. Young and felt indebted to him for the sacrifices he made during the civil rights struggles. Mr. Young had also served with distinction as ambassador to the United Nations under President Carter. Mr. Young had asked me to head his campaign effort in the McDuffie County area.

During the May 8–9, 1990 meeting, the major item of discussion was our long-range planning document. Regent Arthur Gignilliat chaired this committee and we had been meeting, it seemed, forever. The planning document considered creating regional universities and a review of missions at the various colleges and universities. Finally, the document was ready for Board action. Regent John Clark, from the Valdosta area, had problems with our deleting a timeframe, 1992, for Valdosta State's elevation to regional university status. Our fear was that the institution may not have had all of the prerequisites in place, and that state funds would not be available. We agreed to leave the plan on the table for thirty days before taking action. Another controversial issue was whether we would approve a name change for the Home Economics Department at the University of Georgia. In the next ten days, I received forty-seven letters supporting the change. The chancellor recommended a salary increase for all of the presidents and vice chancellors. I vehemently objected to a salary increase for Dr. Jerry Williamson, Gordon College, due to his negative evaluation. I contended that a salary increase for Dr. Williamson would condone the allegations made against him. Following an extensive discussion on this issue, the chancellor withdrew Dr. Williamson's salary increase. I closed my comments by saying that salaries must be reflective of evaluations.

During the June 11–12, 1990 meeting, we reelected Regents Edgar Rhodes and John Henry Anderson chairman and vice-chairman respectively, for a second term. The rationale for a second leadership term was that it takes two years in order to make the desired impact. The Macon community had been lobbying for our changing Macon College's status from a two-year college to four years. I was incensed over the issue. That is, Fort Valley State College was in the service area with an existing four-year program. Yet, Macon College refused to support Fort Valley State College. I sensed that the lack of cooperation from Macon College was racist-based. The regents did not approve their petition despite an emotional appeal from powerful State Representative Denmark Grover, who represented the Macon area. Additionally, Regent John Henry Anderson and I sought to delete 1992 as the target date for the elevation of Valdosta State College to a regional university status. I stated, "It seems to me to be irresponsible, on our part, to convey to this institution that 1992 is firm, when we can only speculate whether state funds will be available at that time ..."

My objection did not prevail; the motion passed by a vote of 8–6. Another controversial issue involved the continued effort to approve a name change for the Home Economics program at the University of Georgia. Following an extended debate, the name change was approved. We also approved a ten-year planning document. I remarked to Regent John Henry Anderson that he and I had lost on most of our dissenting votes. He replied, "That's all right, you must vote your conscience."

As my term on the Board drew to an end, I was beginning to feel a sense of loss ... a feeling of anxiety and emptiness. It dawned on me that come January 1991, I would no longer be a participant in Georgia's premier education policy-making body. Further, it occurred to me that for the first time in twenty years, I would not be involved in education policy. For twenty years, I had participated in education policy-making, perhaps during the most critical time in our nation's history. Beginning with the McDuffie County Board of Education, where I championed full-day kindergarten and self-insurance, to the hiring of more African-Americans, from 19 percent of the teachers to 29 percent, to the Governor's Education Reform Commission, to Chairman of the Board of Regents ... it had been exciting and fulfilling.

As I sat on the stage during the commencement ceremony, Sunday, June 17, 1990, at the Augusta Civic Center during Augusta College's commencement exercise before three to four thousand people, I thought to myself, this may be the last time. I uttered these words of greetings: "On behalf of the Board of Regents, I am pleased to extend our greetings to you on this special occasion. I want to commend Dr. Wallace and the Augusta College faculty for bringing us to another successful commencement ... I deeply appreciate all that you have done for these students. Those of you who are graduating today have made many sacrifices in order to so proudly wear a cap and gown today. I applaud you for your dedication. You represent the pride and promise of an educated society ... However, if that pride and promise is to be fulfilled, you must do all that you can to lift the veil of ignorance from the eyes of so many. As you leave this institution, I hope that you leave with a fire of idealism, a sense of ethics, and a commitment to do all in your power to improve the quality of life for humanity ... Congratulations and best wishes."

I had made similar comments at the Medical College of Georgia commencement program a week earlier Our August 1990 meeting, on the seventh and eighth, centered on our selecting a carrier for the Optional Retirement Plan for system employees. For some reason, I felt a sense of detachment, and not my normal intensity. I felt the effects of being a lame duck. Other agenda items were pretty routine. In the face of declining state revenues, we faced the prospects of having to cut our budget ($1.6 billion) by a considerable amount.

The state of Georgia faced a $300 million shortfall in revenue collections. The Board of Regents had to absorb $31.6 million of the amount. The chancellor, in response to the governor's directive, had reduced our budget 3 percent to 5 percent. We spent a great deal of time agonizing over the cuts. Each regent, while supportive of the chancellor's recommendations, had different approaches. I argued that we should not concede our drastic needs in the face of our fiscal crisis, relative to whether or not we would submit our capital construction list. Regent Barry Phillips took the opposing view. The regents debated the merits of each proposal that was advanced. Finally, Regent Phillips offered a motion that seemed to accommodate most of the budgetary concerns of the regents. I seconded his motion, which passed. Ironically, with declining state revenues, we were expecting an all-time high enrollment in the system of 182 thousand students. In recognition of our budget woes, we canceled our scheduled meeting at Georgia Southwestern College in Americus the next month.

On October 9, 1990, as I left the Radisson Hotel, where I usually stayed during board meetings in Atlanta, and drove down Courtland Street toward the state capitol, I felt a surge of pride and gratitude. To think that God had given me an opportunity to participate and effect policies in education was humbling. In reflecting on these experiences, I felt the presence of my deceased father. My father, who did not live long enough to see any of my accomplishments in education, would have been proud of me.

Our meeting agenda was normal. Regent Lamar Cousins read an appreciation resolution citing Regent Barry Phillips for the role he played in bringing the Olympics to Atlanta in 1996. Regent John Henry Anderson moved and I seconded the motion for the Resolution to be recorded in our minutes. The chancellor reported that our enrollment had reached a record of 180,400 students. The other agenda issues dealt with student immunization and the optional retirement plan for employees.

The December meeting's major focus was on the budget shortfall. In addition to the $31 million cut imposed by Governor Harris, Governor-elect Zell Miller was asking all state agencies to reduce their budgets by an additional 1 percent. For the regents, this meant an additional $9 million. We discussed several alternatives, including a surcharge of $10 per student. After Chancellor Propst discussed this approach with the office of planning and budget, word came back that the Governor-elect Miller would rather we try another approach. Other agenda issues were pretty standard. Regent Jackie Ward and I were in our final month as regents; in this regard, several of our fellow regents expressed the desire that Governor-elect Miller would reappoint us to the board. We had not received any indication of Mr. Miller's plans regarding our status. I would have welcomed another term in order to complete some of the issues that we had not resolved. For instance, I was passionate about increased minority enrollment, greater employment opportunities for minorities, and other issues.

In approaching the Board of Regents' office on January 8, 1991 for our meeting, I felt a deep sense of gratitude. I looked across the street at the gold-domed capitol, and thought how fortunate I had been to serve the citizens of Georgia. As I walked, I prayed a prayer of thanks to God. Upon entering the building, I greeted everyone and kept thinking to myself that this might very well be my last time as a regent. Board Secretary Henry Neal asked me to lead the regents in prayer. I uttered, "Thank you God for the opportunity to serve ... help us to focus on those who are less fortunate ..."

The big news was the resignation of Dr. John Palms as President of Georgia State University in order to accept the presidency at the University of South Carolina. The chancellor gave his state of the University System speech. I felt good about his speech as well as his obvious commitment to full access to minority students and personnel. Although we had suffered a $40 million budget cut, the chancellor's plan was to minimize the harm to students.

As we closed our meeting on Wednesday, Regents Arthur Gignilliat, James Brown, Bill Turner, and others expressed the hope that the new governor-elect, Zell Miller, would reappoint me to the Board. As Regent Jackie Ward and I embraced, her eyes glistened with tears. It really had been a wonderful experience. I had grown so much during the seven years, I had learned so much ... but there was so much more to learn. I thanked God for the experience!

When I returned to my office at the Pilgrim Health and Life Insurance Company from a speaking engagement at South Georgia College in Douglas, Georgia, I returned a phone call to Regent Jackie Ward. She informed me that House Speaker Tom Murphy had informed Regent Edgar Rhodes that two new regents had been selected to replace us on the Board of Regents. I was surprised to a degree—I felt that I would be reappointed. Regent Jackie Ward suggested that I call Regent Rhodes, Chairman of the Board of Regents, for confirmation. Regent Rhodes confirmed the message from the governor via Speaker Murphy. I felt a little empty and hollow on the inside. However, I felt that God's plan would prevail and that he was not through with me yet.

The days following my being replaced were pretty agonizing mentally. I felt a degree of depression and emptiness. The days turned into weeks, and finally I began to feel much better. I kept telling myself how fortunate I had been to rise from obscurity to center stage ... from the cotton fields to statewide office. I finally accepted the fact that following twenty years in education policy-making, my tenure was over and there would be other challenges to meet.

In reflection, I looked back with pride in having championed the following causes:

- State education critical issues
- Strategic planning for the University System
- Desegregation / increased accessibility for minorities
- Increased funding for Augusta College and the Medical College of Georgia
- Improved procedures for presidential searches

In leaving the office that I had held for the past seven years, I felt that the state of education had benefited from my tenure. The quality of life was a little better for Georgians and I had grown immensely.

The tradition of the Board of Regents was to host a reception-dinner in honor of departing regents. Regents, along with the chancellor, would make reflective comments similar to a roast on mutually shared experiences on the years of working together. The departing regent would also make reflective comments in the form of a lighthearted roast toward his fellow regents. My comments toward my fellow regents followed at the reception on November 21, 1991:

> My years on the Board of Regents were very rewarding and offered me experiences that I will never forget.
> For example:
> Chairman Edgar Rhodes, who is a highly respected man. Who would ever guess that our illustrious Chairman would lock his wife in the Reynolds Plantation house on Sapelo Island? I can hear his wife, Daisy, as though it were yesterday, screaming "Help, help, please rescue me." (During a regents' retreat meeting at the Reynolds Plantation house on St. Simon's Island, Regent Rhodes and his wife, Daisy, accidentally locked themselves in their room. My wife and I were in the next room and heard Daisy's plea for help. I was able to force the jammed door open.)

I can remember my dear friend Jackie Ward saying, "Dad-gummit, Chancellor, how much longer are we going to tolerate this issue with Georgia Military College? Although it's in my own hometown it has to clean up its act." (Regent Jackie Ward, who grew up in Milledgeville, Georgia, where Georgia Military College is located, often chided the chancellor for permitting Georgia Military College to sidestep certain budgetary restraints. She frequently used the words "dad-gum-mit" to vent her frustrations.)

I can remember John Henry for challenging us to run the University System as a sole commissioner runs his county: lean and mean ... and don't sell any land, especially in Bartow County where the price of land was extremely expensive. (Regent John Henry Anderson, the sole commissioner in his home county, Pulaski, was often accused of attempting to manage the university system as though it were a county.)

I remember Arthur Gignilliat vetoing all architects ... except those from Savannah. (Regent Gignilliat was often chided by his fellow regents for being highly critical of architects, unless they were from the Savannah area, where he lived.)

I remember Elridge McMillian's propensity to send all regents and staff to the dictionary to discover that he had called us bumbling buffoons. (Regent Eldridge McMillian had a mastery of speech that few could rival; his eloquent dialogue would often leave us speechless.)

I hear John Robinson's call for the University System to scrap our heritage ... and put everything on a global basis, so that all University System decisions would be tempered by global economics and market forces. (Regent John Robinson's tendency to globalize issues was frequently noted by his fellow regents.)

I will remember Lamar Cousins, who has to be related to Elridge McMillan for his ability to command complete silence with his oratorical skills. I never understood why he became a physician rather than a college English professor. (Regent Lamar Cousin, a physician, commanded the eloquence of Regent McMillian in our deliberations.) I will always remember our chancellor for inviting us to his home for dinner … but he never cooked collard greens, black-eyed peas, candied yams, and ham hocks. Instead, he would serve us Kentucky Fried Chicken in buckets. (Chancellor Dean Propst would on special occasions host the regents for dinner at his home. I often teased him about not serving soul food.)

I will always remember Henry Neal's ability to always manage to find the most inexpensive place to eat. (Henry Neal, Executive Secretary, was noted for being tight-fisted with money. He would walk several blocks in order to find an inexpensive restaurant.)

Seriously, in all of my years of public service, thirteen years on a local school board, eighteen months as a member of the Governor's Education Review commission, I have not met a more unselfish group of dedicated public servants, who have contributed so much to so many. My life is richer and fuller because of my years of association with you.

Barney and I will always cherish the value of your friendship.

We wish you the very best as you continue to serve the citizens of our great state.

THANK YOU SO MUCH.

# THE FINAL CHAPTER

THE ROAD FROM THE cotton fields in Emanuel County, Georgia to the various governing boards has not been an easy one. The route was paved with many failures and disappointments. There were times when I wanted to give up and quit, because in many instances the rules of the game were unfair and designed for my failure.

When I was tempted to quit, I reflected on my rich heritage. A heritage uprooted from the soil of the African continent and planted in the soil of this great country. My ancestors' roots are deeply planted in the soil of this nation's past, present, and future. By the sweat of the brow, the shedding of blood, my ancestors carved a place in American history. A rich heritage that helped this nation rise to unparalleled power and greatness. So quitting was not an option for me because I had the presence of God and my ancestors pointing the way through the treacherous journey of life.

In those instances when my route took me through the hurdles of second-class treatment, I reflected on my grandfather Winder's resolve to leave a rich legacy of determination for his descendants to use as guideposts. Imagine, barely out of slavery and the sharecropping experience, my grandfather was able to acquire a relatively large plot of land and to retain its title in a hostile environment. As my uncle James often said to me, the Greene family believes in taking the 't out of the word can't, and when you do that, you discover that you can.

As a child, I learned the value of hard work and public service from my father. The construction of the Cross-Greene school by my father and other relatives in the community left an indelible impression on me about the rewards of hard work. I saw men of meager means build an institution that would affect the lives of future generations. I saw my father and uncles build a fledgling school that represented the pride and promise of the future. These strong men often visited the school as volunteers, attending the PTA meetings and various school functions to dramatize their support. Their unselfish commitment to my future removed any notion of quitting from my bones.

As I left the Cross-Greene community at the age of eighteen to strike out on my own, with thirty-five dollars that I had saved from picking cotton, along with millions of dollars in aspirations, I always knew that I was not alone. God's presence directed my path as I traveled the road of uncertainty. He stationed people along the route to shepherd my route. It was no accident that M. M. Scott took my hand and led me through the first hurdle of employment. He then passed me on to a team of quality people in the Thomson community in the Long family. The Long family treated me as though I was biologically connected to them. This connection led me to the Springfield Baptist Church, where the Reverend J. H. West provided spiritual guidance. God's guiding hand led me to my wife and a successful marriage of more than forty years.

With a deep sense of humility and gratitude, I have been able to travel the long road from the cotton fields in Emanuel County to various boardrooms. In this regard, I have never forgotten from where I have traveled and the incumbent stewardship of unselfish service as I close the final chapter.

# APPENDIX 1

## SELECTED BOARDS

1. McDuffie County Selective Service*
   (1969–1972)
2. Ten-Sixties Advisory Board*
   (1969–1973)
3. McDuffie County Board of Education*
   (1970–1983)
4. United Way of McDuffie County—President*
   (1978–1979)
5. State Health Planning Board
   (1979–1983)
6. Georgia Constitution Revision Commission*
   (1978–1979)
7. Governor's Education Review Commission
   (1982–1983)
8. University System of Georgia Board of Regent
   (1984–1991)
9. Georgia Post Secondary Board of Directors*
   (1984–1985)
10. Thomson-McDuffie Chamber Board of Directors
    (1985–1987)
11. Metro-Augusta Chamber Board of Directors
    (1991–1994)
12. McDuffie Bank and Trust (First Bank)*
    (1989–present)

13. Blue Cross / Blue Shield of Georgia
    (1993–2001)
14. Southeastern Technology Board of Directors
    (1996–2002)
15. Morris Museum Board of Directors
    (1996–2003)
16. National Science Center Board of Directors
    (1996–present)
17. St. Joseph Hospital Foundation Board of Directors
    (1989–1996)
18. Pilgrim H. & L. Insurance Company Board of Directors
    (1979–1990)
19. National Insurance Association Board of Directors
    (1987–1989)
20. CSRA Community Foundation*
    (1999-present)
21. Healthcare Georgia Foundation
    (2000–present)
22. Rotary Club of Augusta*
    (2000–present)


* First African-American

# APPENDIX 2

## HONORS AND AWARDS

THROUGH THE YEARS I have received many awards and citations, all of which I am grateful for. The following is a list of some of them:

- "Outstanding Young Man of the Year" Thomson Jaycees
- "Man of the Year" Thomson Progressive Civic Club
- "Who's Who Among Black Leaders" National Urban League
- "Who's Who Among Students In American Universities and Colleges"
- "Georgia's Governor Club"
- "Honorary Mayor" designation Baton Rogue, Louisiana
- "Honorary Citizen" destination Mobile, Alabama
- "Colonel Aide De Camp" Governor Jimmy Carter, Georgia
- "Colonel Aide De Camp" Governor George Busbee, Georgia
- "Colonel Aide De Camp" Governor Joe Frank Harris, Georgia
- "Colonel Aide De Camp" Governor Edwin Edwards, Louisiana
- "Marketing Officer of the Year" National Insurance Association
- "Outstanding Faculty Award" Augusta State University

- "Business Person of the Year" CSRA Business League
- "1987 Distinguished Alumnus Award" Augusta College
- "1989 Distinguished Alumnus Award" University of Georgia

# APPENDIX 3

MINUTES OF THE MEETING OF THE
BOARD OF REGENTS OF THE UNIVERSITY SYSTEM OF GEORGIA
HELD IN
ATLANTA, GEORGIA

June 13-14, 1989

Pursuant to a call letter issued on June 7, 1989, the Board of Regents of the University System of Georgia met on Tuesday, June 13, at 1:00 P.M., and again on Wednesday, June 14, 1989, at 9:00 A.M., in the Board offices at 244 Washington Street, S.W., in Atlanta, Georgia.

The meeting was called to order by Chairman Joseph D. Greene.

The invocation was given by Regent William B. Turner on June 13, and by Regent Arthur M. Gignilliat, Jr. on June 14.

Members of the Board present were as follows:

Present: Regents Joseph D. Greene - June 13-14, 1989
John Henry Anderson, Jr. - June 13-14, 1989
James E. Brown - June 13-14, 1989
John Howard Clark - June 13-14, 1989
W. Lamar Cousins - June 13-14, 1989
Thomas H. Frier, Sr. - June 13-14, 1989
Arthur M. Gignilliat, Jr. - June 13-14, 1989
Elridge W. McMillan - June 13-14, 1989
Barry Phillips - June 13-14, 1989
Edgar L. Rhodes - June 13-14, 1989
John W. Robinson, Jr. - June 13, 1989
William B. Turner - June 13-14, 1989
Jackie M. Ward - June 13-14, 1989
Carolyn D. Yancey - June 13-14, 1989

Absent: Regents John W. Robinson, Jr. - June 14, 1989
Deen Day Smith - June 13-14, 1989

Chairman Greene stated that Regent Robinson had previously requested that he be excused from the meeting of the Board on June 14, and that Regent Smith had requested to be excused from the meeting of the Board on June 13-14. For reasons deemed sufficient by the Chairman, Regents Robinson and Smith were excused.

\*\*\*

Upon motion properly made, variously seconded and unanimously adopted, the Board approved the minutes of the meeting of the Board of Regents held on May 9-10, 1989.

# INDEX

124 — Joseph D. Greene

Stephens County Hospital, 24
Stillmore, GA, 5
Summertown, GA, 5
Summerville Neighborhood Organization, 80
Swain, Mr., 6
Swainsboro High, 6
Swainsboro, Georgia, 2–5

Tedesco, Dr. Fran, 39, 85–87
Ten-Sixties Advisory Board, 49
The Baptist Training Union, 15
Thomas, Lena, 89
Thomas, Mr., principal, 4
Thompson, Hattie, 13–14
Thomson, GA, 14
Toccoa, GA, 23
Tolbert, Fred, 66
Trigon Healthcare, Inc., 67
Trotter, Dr. Virginia, 79
Trust Company Bank, 72
Turner, Bill, 94, 106
Twin City, GA, 5
Tyler, Rev. L. M., 20
Tyson, Grace, 89

Underwood, Charlie, 70
United States Army, 25
United States Selective Service Draft Board, 25
United Way of Thomson-McDuffie County, 50
University of Georgia, 33–34, 79
University System of Georgia, 31

Valdosta State College, 103
Vansickle, 27
Vereen, Jerry, 66
Vietnam War, 25, 27

Volkswagen, 23

Wadley, GA, 6
Wagener, SC, 19, 21
Walker, Dr. Ralph, 33
Walker, S. W., 52
Walker, Solomon II, 35, 38, 62
Wallace, Dr. Richard, 39, 82
Ward, Jackie, 78, 81–83, 85
Wellpoint Insurance Company, 67
West, Clara, 15, 89
West, Reverend J. H., 15, 112
Wheeler, Mr. Lloyd, 36
Whitehead Street, 16, 20
Who's Who Among Students in American Colleges and Universities, 33
Widener, Jack, 68–69
Williams, Dr. Roscoe, 32
Williamson, Dr. Jerry, 100–102
Wilson, Robert Jr., 73
Wilson, Robert Sr., 73
Wingfield, Reverend G. H., 13
Wright, Deloris, 42

Yancey, Carolyn, 84, 94
Young, Andrew, 101
Young, Bennye, 73

Printed in the United States
76460LV00004B/103-162

9 781587 364600